FOOTSTEPS
THROUGH TULSA

Marilyn Inhofe-Tucker,
Sandy Jones and Kate Reeves

Marilyn Inhofe-Tucker

FOOTSTEPS THROUGH TULSA L.L.C.

PUBLISHED BY
Footsteps Through Tulsa L.L.C.
1398 East 25th Street,
Tulsa, Oklahoma 74114

The following books were quoted or relied upon:

City of Tulsa's Urban Development Department. The 1992 Tulsa Historic Preservation Plan Report.

Debo, Angie. *From Creek Town to Oil Capital.*

Dunn, Nina. *Tulsa's Magic Roots.*

Ellsworth, Scott. *Death in a Promised Land.*

Irving, Washington. *Tour on the Prairies.*

Logsdon, Guy. *The University of Tulsa.*

Silvey, Larry, and Drown, Douglas F. (editors) *Tulsa Spirit.*

Inhofe-Tucker, Marilyn. *The History of the Samuel H. Kress Foundation's Dispersal of Renaissance Paintings and Sculpture. . .* (Masters Thesis, available in libraries at The Philbrook Museum of Art and The University of Tulsa.)

We express our appreciation to all those who graciously helped with the information in this book. We especially would like to express our appreciation to our husbands Bob Jones and Ralph Tucker, who enthusiastically encouraged us by typing, walking, and listening.

PRINTED IN THE UNITED STATES OF AMERICA

DESIGN BY CAROL HARALSON
COVER PAINTING BY RUTH ARMSTRONG
DRAWINGS BY KATE REEVES

DEDICATED TO THE
VOLUNTEERS OF
TULSA, WHO THROUGH
THEIR VISION AND
TIRELESS EFFORTS
MADE TULSA A
THRIVING AND
BEAUTIFUL CITY

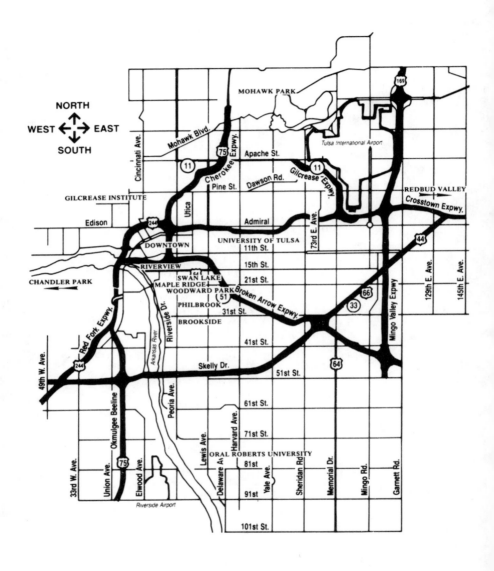

F O R E W O R D

GRACIOUS TO THE FOOT TRAVELER, the city of Tulsa offers an interesting and rich array of things to see, and a wonderful setting for seeing them. Stylish shopping centers, excellent museums, universities, and elegant residential neighborhoods nestle quietly in seasonal glory. Downtown, there is the bustle of a major urban center, with gleaming skyscrapers shouldering historic buildings. Nature trails educate and entertain in the appreciation they provide for the area's inherent beauty. Threads of Indian heritage and oil boom days are still visible in the historical fabric of the city.

Walking is the unsurpassed means by which to experience all that Tulsa has to offer. It provides the leisure to contemplate the enigmatic questions associated with stately mansions lining tree-shaded streets. It allows careful and intimate appreciation of horticultural masterpieces painstakingly nourished by talented hands. As the title suggests, the walker also follows the footsteps of early Tulsans—some of whom appear prominently in the city's chronicle; others supply history with nothing more than daily life. Together, they provide the past, resurrected in the city's skyline, neighborhoods, and parks. As you walk through Tulsa, you can applaud the vision for beauty and preservation of the beautiful.

Whether you are a first-time visitor, a long-time resident, or somewhere in between, the walks in this book suggest scenic and enjoyable routes to follow. They provide helpful background information on Tulsa's vegetation, architecture, museums, and historical past. They take you everywhere from famous visitor attractions to secluded residential neighborhoods.

None of the tours are strenuous, and all can easily be walked in a morning or an afternoon. For safety reasons, walking in groups is suggested, especially in urban areas. At the beginning of each walk you will find a note on its distance and the approximate walking time. Assuming that you will be driving a car to the starting point (for bus information call (918) 584-6421), each walk begins at an easy to locate spot, with parking at least adequate, and usually plentiful. All routes make a loop, thereby returning you to your car.

Although the architectural and historical walks are loosely in chronological order, consideration of seasonal conditions is advised for all walks. For instance, nature walks can be unbearable in summer heat; choose instead a museum or downtown tour where escape from heat is possible. Radiant colors of spring and fall make those seasons premier touring times. Tulsa's mild wintry weather is also conducive to walking. After selecting the walk that appeals to you, put on a comfortable pair of shoes and begin to enjoy the physically and mentally curative pleasures of walking.

CONTENTS

Riverview

THE RIVERVIEW NEIGHBORHOOD, listed on the
Oklahoma Landmark's inventory as a state historical
district, has five structures and one site on the National
Register of Historic Places. Interspersed with high-rise
construction and the new apartments are remnants of Tulsa's
past, authenticating now legendary people and events. These
physical fragments, in concert with historical information and
imagination, bring to life the epoch story of a Creek town
becoming the Oil Capital of the World.

Holy Trinity Greek Orthodox Church at 1222 South
Guthrie Avenue hosts the Greek Holiday festival in September.
It features Greek food, music, and dancing. During the event,
the church is open for tours; otherwise, call (918) 583-0417 if
you wish to view the interior.

*To begin the tour, park in the River Park's lot just north of 21st
at Riverside Drive. Picnicking facilities are near the parking lot.*

The walk begins on Cheyenne Avenue; therefore, cross
Riverside Drive to 19th Street and walk to Cheyenne. Turn left
(north) and walk to **1802 South Cheyenne**. James Alexander
Veasey, founder of Holland Hall School, arrived in Tulsa to be a
lawyer for the Dawes Commission. In 1912 he built this home
where he lived until 1938, when he retired as Chief Counsel of
Carter Oil Company, a subsidiary of Standard Oil Company of
New Jersey. Originally he had planned to build a brick home,
but he was short of cash. Instead of stone quoins on the corners, he instructed the builder to put wood, a constant reminder
of his more humble beginnings. An excellent example of

DISTANCE
2 miles
TIME
1.5 hours

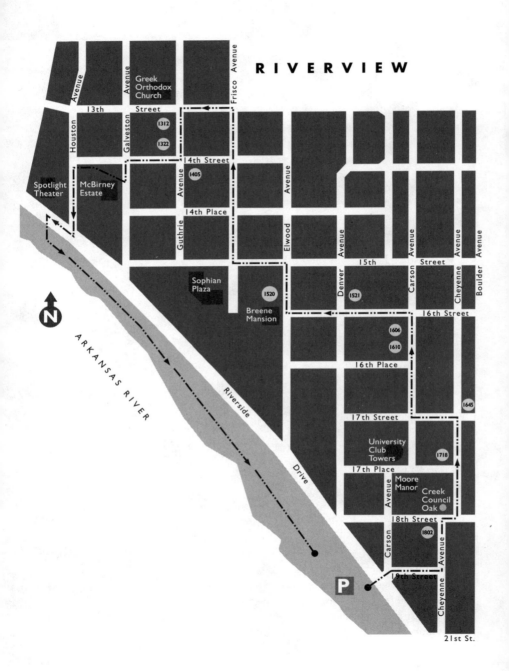

R I V E R V I E W

Colonial Revival style, the Veasey house exhibits the Greek simplicity of detailing and ancient motifs of dentil moldings and
Doric columns underneath a pediment, all hallmarks of this
style. Notice the dormer with traceried windows.

CREEK NATION COUNCIL OAK PARK. Across 18th Street
is Creek Nation Council Oak Park. The **Council Oak tree,** an
historical monument, has witnessed events in Tulsa since the
first inhabitants in 1836. On this site, the crest of a low, wooded
hill overlooking the Arkansas River, the Lochapoka clan of
Creeks ended their tortuous migration from Alabama. With a
United States Militia escort, they had moved westward through
Mississippi and Tennessee to Memphis, thence by steamboat
(down the Mississippi, up the Arkansas) to Little Rock. There,
low water forced them to disembark. With pack ponies for their
meager possessions and supplies, they walked the final 300 miles
to their new homeland. It was a slow and painful trek, and of
the original 630 men, women, and children, 161 died en route.

Nevertheless, the 1836 arrival was marked with a solemn
and traditional ceremony. A large oak towered over them as a
Creek brave, Achee Yahola, deposited the sacred coals kept alive
on the long march. As Angie Debo wrote, "It was a strange
beginning for a modern city—the flickering fire, the silent valley, the dark intent faces, and the wild cadences of the ritual."

A traditional "busking ground" was soon laid out with ceremonial exactness. Around a large, cleared space stood four council sheds that formed a square with the oak in the southeast corner. The "busk," usually held in July, was the most important
ceremony for the purpose of conducting tribal business and giving thanks for the new crop of green corn. The Creeks kindled a
"new fire" in the center of the square, performed dances and
bathed in a creek that lay to the east. Tribal members were for-
bidden to eat roasting ears until this rite had been observed.
(George Perryman [Brookside Walk] as a courtesy to
Lochapoka, his wife's town, often contributed beef or a hog, and
on one never-forgotten occasion he furnished a whole case of
Star tobacco.) "For a mile up and down the river could be heard
the rhythmic beat of drum and song, and dancing feet."

The site was used ceremoniously as late as 1896 with state-

> *"It was a strange beginning for a modern city — the flickering fire, the silent valley, the dark intent faces, and the wild cadences of the ritual."*
>
> ANGIE DEBO

Creek Council Oak Tree

THE "HANGIN' TREE"

The Council Oak is known to some as the "Hangin' Tree." The details of this "ceremony" are buried with William G. Bruner, late member of the Creek House of Kings. He died in 1952 and was the son of parents who migrated to Oklahoma from Alabama with the Creek Tribe. As a boy, Bruner played under the shade of the Council Oak Tree, and one memorable day witnessed the hanging of three men convicted of cattle rustling. The hanging limb is identified as one twelve feet above the ground.

hood in 1907 marking the end of the Creek Nation. So strong was the tradition of the area, however, that the Creek Council Oak was identified, largely through the efforts of the Daughters of the American Revolution, and carefully preserved. The tree is a mature post oak standing approximately 75 feet in height with the high limb span measuring 85 feet. Thirteen feet in circumference at its base with bark one and one half inches thick, the tree is still growing according to core sampling. One expert expressed the opinion that the tree likely grew to a size larger than normal for post oaks because its roots tapped the nearby spring water (now underground) that originally ran beside the first chief's (Yahola) cabin. For protection the tree is fitted with lightning rods (visible in late fall and winter), and the park is maintained with traditional Native American plantings of cotton, pumpkin, tobacco, and corn, as well as herbs.

CHEYENNE AVENUE. Walk to the park's sign, and turn left (north) on Cheyenne Avenue. Now concentrate on another historic Tulsa era—the oil boom—which provided the money for this neighborhood, Riverview. Residential construction in this area encompassed the years 1907 until 1920. During that time, the United States entered World War I, and the Oklahoma oil boom entered its finest hour with one-third of the world's petroleum produced by the fields of Oklahoma. The oil boom corresponded to Tulsa's major period of growth from a town of 1,390 people in 1900 to 78,580 only twenty years later. An oil man's empire included the best house money could buy as illustrated by this neighborhood. The owners of these fine homes were among the founders of Tulsa, often men who started with a few dollars and buffeted by fate, acumen, and risk made vast fortunes. Aside from many locally famous persons, owners of these properties included Waite Phillips, E. W. Sinclair, and W. G. Skelly. The area showed its silk-stocking character when in 1923 Harry Sinclair's horse, Bev, won the Kentucky Derby, and Josh Cosden's horse, Martingale, finished second.

Many residential styles of architecture are represented in Riverview—pockets of bungalows, cottages, and mansions. Adaptations of Spanish and Georgian Revival are seen on the tree-lined streets. **1718 South Cheyenne Avenue** presents a

Tulsa translation of the Greek Revival style. The builder, George Bole, built the home for his family in 1917 and brought artisans from Italy for its construction. In 1926, Bole sold the home and founded the addition of Bolewood Acres. The subsequent and only other resident presented the house to his wife as a wedding gift.

The northeast corner of 17th Street and Cheyenne Avenue, **1645 South Cheyenne Avenue,** was once the home of C. J. Wrightsman, one of the last of the early day wildcatters. Wrightsman, who arrived in Tulsa in 1906, made oil, legal, and political history during his dynamic career. An attorney and territorial senator, Wrightsman was one of the authorities on Indian land leases and oil legislation. In fact, he was the originator of the depletion allowance for oil, gas, and other mineral production. In an unsuccessful bid for the United States Senate in 1930, Wrightsman was championed by most of the "best people." Though considered incorruptible, he lost popular support by his avowal that wealth was necessary for public service—a "gentleman" could not live on a politician's salary. His wealth worked against him politically, and Wrightsman aggravated the

1645 South
Cheyenne Avenue

situation with misplaced homilies about his butler dispensing handouts from his mansion's back door. The mansion, unusual in the use of so much glass, is built on a base of native stone. The trim displays the talent and artistry of the craftsmen of the time, especially evident in the scallops over the front door.

CARSON AVENUE. Turn west on 17th Street and continue one block to Carson Avenue. **Moore Manor**, especially visible through the bare trees of winter, is located a block off the route to the left (south). Completed in 1918, the house is considered to be the finest example of neo-Colonial residential architecture built during the early oil boom years with its Palladian windows, Corinthian columns, and Georgian Revival cornices. Frank L. Moore started business as a small drilling contractor and parlayed a few drilling interests into an empire. With his new found wealth, he constructed Moore Manor, which his son, four years old at the time, remembers as being "way out in the country."

One-and two-story houses of stucco, brick, clapboard, and a variety of roofing materials have been somewhat over-shadowed by high-rise apartment construction at the corner of 17th Street and Carson Avenue. The circular apartments, **University Club Towers**, are on the site of what was once the "showplace of Tulsa." It was the second home in this immediate area belonging to Josh Cosden and had, in 1916, one of the first indoor swimming pools in the state and the first lighted tennis courts with imported English clay. (The apartment tennis courts, located on the west side of the new high rise, are in the same location.)

Turn right and begin walking north. Carson Street, once part of the subdivision Carlton Place, remains as one of the most intact residential streets in the area. This street, developed by John Blair, a Tulsa architect (Mapleridge Walks I and II), was the newest and most fashionable residential area in 1909. It drew Brady Heights oilmen and newcomers through its two red brick archways at 14th Street and Cheyenne Avenue and 14th Street and Carson Avenue. Only part of the gateway at 14th Street and Carson remains, but it is a strong visual reminder.

1610 South Carson Avenue was the early home of Robert M. McFarlin. As an early day Oklahoma cattleman, later

With its Palladian windows, Corinthian columns, and Georgian Revival cornices, Moore House is considered to be the finest example of neo-Colonial residential architecture built during the early oil boom years.

branching into the oil and banking business, McFarlin generally is credited with playing a major role in Tulsa's early development. He was probably more active than any other one man in establishing, in 1910, the former Exchange National Bank, now the Bank of Oklahoma (Downtown Walk I). McFarlin's name is still recognized in Tulsa for his philanthropy (University of Tulsa Walk). A September 28, 1915 copy of the *Daily Democrat* (precursor of *The Tulsa Tribune*) states that the home was constructed by Blair Brothers and sold for the price of $13,500. Architecturally, the residence is noted for its gracious front porch; the proportions and mass of the house may be familiar, but the porch is uniquely spectacular. The great stone Doric columns, crowned with a more delicate stone balustrade, create rhythm and harmony echoing classical influence. The home is now the McCormack Photography Studio, and the McCormacks are extremely accommodating in allowing parts of the interior to be viewed if the facilities are not being used for a photographic session.

Porch, 1610 South Carson Avenue

(The studio is open weekdays, 9 to 5:30.) Enter the south entrance of the porch and check with the receptionist. She will direct you through the living room to the Wedgewood Room. Designed by the Josiah Wedgewood Company (Philbrook Museum of Art Walk), famed for its pottery, the ceiling and trim were shipped in sections from England.

The McFarlins' daughter and son-in-law, the J. A. Chapmans, lived next door at **1606 South Carson Avenue** in the home originally owned by Josh Cosden. Constructed in 1912 of the finest materials

J. A. CHAPMAN
A Private Man

Along with his father-in-law and partners in the McMan Oil and Gas Company, J. A. Chapman is said to have been involved in production of oil in practically all the major fields in Oklahoma. However, due perhaps to Chapman's private nature (and his reputed allergy to cigarette smoke) Chapman and his wife seldom went out in society. A very charitable man, he preferred to give to private organizations that received little or no funds (University of Tulsa Walk). At the time of his death in 1966, the Chapman fortune went entirely to charity; it was estimated to be $100 million. Earlier he was quoted as saying, "I'm doing this for people, not for publicity."

available at a cost of $12,000, it was the most expensive residence to that date in Tulsa. As mentioned earlier in the walk, Cosden, Tulsa's most illustrious oilman, later built another home farther south on Carson Avenue. However, this home must have meant the start of a life of leisure to Ottille, Cosden's first wife, for she moved here from a one-room shack they had occupied while Cosden built his fledgling refinery business.

Especially in late fall and winter, the view from various points in Riverview to the refinery, once Cosden's (Downtown Walk I), on the west bank of the Arkansas River still seems to link the anachronistic oil mansions to the present.

The next occupant of 1606 was J. A. Chapman, married to Leta May McFarlin. At 16th Street and Carson Avenue, turn left (west) and continue a block to Denver Avenue. Many of these residential homes have been converted into offices or other adaptive uses.

DENVER AVENUE. Before crossing Denver Avenue, look at an appreciably smaller, but delightfully styled, blue house on the northeast corner at **1521 South Denver.** Often described as Cape Cod, the house is actually more Greek Revival style with its columns and clean architectural lines.

ELWOOD AVENUE. Once across Denver Avenue, continue straight (west) on 16th Street to Elwood Avenue. Turn left (south) for a few feet to view the Breene Mansion. Luxury cars of the early 1900s are easy to imagine whizzing around the driveway of **1608 South Elwood Avenue,** home of oilman Frank Breene. Built in 1918 after Breene's European travels, it is a replica, though smaller, of a country manor that Emperor Napoleon built for Josephine. The formal gardens of the estate also continued the French theme. Constructed for $100,000, the eighteen-room house was elegantly furnished with seven marble fireplaces. Frank Breene was a prominent businessman of his day, coming as many others did from the Pennsylvania and Ohio oil fields. His background and experience in the older areas of production assured him a position in Oklahoma among the list of largest operators. His daughter, Grayce, who later married Senator Robert S. Kerr, spent much of her childhood in this privileged atmosphere.

In 1959, the house was once again in the spotlight with charity rising out of the ashes of faded elegance. Magi Kimball, an acquaintance of the Kerrs, opened a school in the mansion for mentally handicapped children. The school, staffed completely by volunteers, operated at this location for twenty-five years. Mrs. Kimball had campaigned for President Kennedy and corresponded with him, and the generous-hearted enterprise bore the name John F. Kennedy School for Seizure Children. Today, with its rigid symmetry, Palladian windows, Doric columns, and contrast of red brick with white trim, the house is considered a fine example of Georgian Colonial architecture.

1521 South Denver Avenue

Retrace your steps and head north on Elwood Avenue. Notice the small, yet distinctive house next to the Breene Mansion. The two houses are as great a contrast in style as they are in size. The opposite of grand or imposing, the residence at **1520 South Elwood Avenue,** with its door completely hidden from view, makes a statement of privacy and charm in its English cottage architecture.

FRISCO AVENUE Turn left (west) on 15th Street and walk a block to Frisco Avenue. Straight ahead is the **Sophian Plaza.** Dr. Sophian of Kansas City constructed this eight-story project in 1925 to be a twin of another Sophian Plaza in Kansas City. Very formal, with its brick dressed in limestone and Italianate details, the Sophian lived up to its reputation described at the time as being an apartment complex "the type and style of which was only found in the large cities." Converted in 1978 to condominiums, the Sophian features elegant, spacious rooms with high ceilings and elaborate moldings. This living arrangement, so close to downtown, is popular with both the established wealthy and the younger career professionals who are restoring the building to its old world splendor.

Proceed right (north) on Frisco Avenue for three blocks. This street was made wider than usual to accommodate trolly tracks. On 13th Street turn left (west) and continue to Guthrie Avenue. The **Holy Trinity Greek Orthodox Church** is on the northwest corner at 1222 South Guthrie Avenue. Appearing quite modern, the church is actually the square shape of ancient Byzantine architecture. Stone or marble are the traditional materials of this style; however, this building was constructed with consideration for both the European heritage of the church and Oklahoma's current material market. Thus, contemporary brick adorns the dome-topped Byzantine structure.

Sophian Plaza

GUTHRIE AVENUE. Turn left (south) on Guthrie Avenue. A tile roof, wide overhang, and Italianate details and embossing show a Mediterranean influence which characterizes the home at **1312 South Guthrie.** Patrick M. Kerr, an oil refiner who later lost his fortune in 1929, was the first owner.

Apart from the obvious luxury of large-sized homes such as this, Riverview boasted another luxury—accessibility. Today, Tulsans commuting from the heavily-trafficked areas to the business center of Tulsa are envious of the short distance from Riverview to downtown. An earlier occupant of this home recalls, "No one thought of driving to work, and we could watch our children walk to school." (Riverview School was located just across from the Greek Orthodox Church.) In the days before shopping centers, all necessities and luxuries Tulsa had to offer were just a few blocks away.

The first owner of the next home at **1322 South Guthrie** was Lee Clinton, member of a family that figured heavily in the early days of Tulsa. (His sister married J. H. McBirney; his brother, Dr. Fred Clinton, drilled the first oil well in Redfork providing the spur for torrential speculation in the Tulsa area.) Lee Clinton was active in Tulsa banking; he founded Union National Bank, which later became First National Bank and Trust Company of Tulsa. W. G. Skelly persuaded Clinton to become president of the Tulsa stockyards in 1934. Clinton's home, built in 1920, was designed by George Winkler, who was also the architect of Holy Family Cathedral, Central High School, and the Mayo Hotel (Downtown Walks I and II). Reminiscent of a New England Christmas card, the home reflects Georgian and Federal influences. The front entry is embellished with a fanlight, side windows, and recessed panelling of pre-Civil War vintage, which Mrs. Clinton spotted at a New Orleans French Quarter demolition site and had shipped by rail to Tulsa. The house has fifteen rooms, including a full basement where the Clintons' domestic help made soap and tended to the laundry. Their black cook was hidden there during the 1921 race riot (Greenwood Walk) to ensure her safety. The home has an electrically operated well that served as an early-day water supply. Since Arkansas River water was considered unfit to drink, only the plumbing operated on river water. The pine trees which now tower above the three-story house were a mistake; the Clintons had ordered dwarf pines. A site of lavish parties and distinguished visitors ranging from W. G. Skelly to Amelia Earhart (a classmate of Clinton's niece), the home was kept in the Clinton family until 1973.

Diagonally across the street from the Clinton home is **1405 South Guthrie Avenue**, once the residence of Nelle Shields

LEE CLINTON: First Man to Cross the Arkansas River by Bridge

Lee Clinton was the first man to cross the Arkansas River by bridge upon its opening in 1904, an event he remembered vividly all his life. "I should," he said. "It put me out of business!" Clinton was part owner of a gas-driven ferry at the Eleventh Street crossing. The old ferry was a side-wheeler that held four wagons and had been operated first by Lincoln Postoak, who gave up the business after the ferry became stuck on a sand bar. He sold the boat to Lee Clinton and his partners, who waited for the river to rise and the ferry to float free.

NELLE SHIELDS JACKSON: How the Note Wasn't Called

Miss Jackson's name, which became synonymous with elegance and good taste, has not escaped some of the anecdotes connected with the city's history. During the Depression, a bank threatened to call her note. It is said that Miss Jackson strode into the meeting of the bank's board of directors and addressing the gentlemen one by one, began, "If your wife, Mr. President, will pay the bill she owes me, and you Mr. . . ., if you'll take care of the little bill Mrs. . . . has over at my shop, and if I can collect from [this one] and [that one], I can meet the note with no trouble." The note wasn't called.

Jackson, ultimately the owner of the exclusive Miss Jackson's store in Utica Square Shopping Center. Nelle came with her mother to Tulsa in 1907 from Pittsburgh, Pennsylvania. Miss Jackson's first position in Tulsa was with Vandevers, then the Beane-Vandever Dry Goods Company. The genesis of Miss Jackson's department store was a small shop, located on the balcony of a jewelry store. After several moves, the shop of her dreams became a reality when it opened in the Philtower Building in 1928. A grand gala introduced the shop to the city. World-famous models showed clothes by foremost American and French designers. Old Georgian silver and Gainsborough portraits were exhibited, and a string quartet from New York City played to everyone's delight. Her home is a New England clapboard two-story, nestled under spreading trees behind a neatly trimmed hedge. In Miss Jackson's day, the wood was of a saffron hue that appealed to her particularly. Those familiar with her shop can readily believe that the interior must have been characterized by dignified richness and grace. In the entrance hall is a wide staircase, the hand rails of which were upholstered in apricot velvet.

GALVESTON AVENUE. Turn right (west) on 14th Street and walk to Galveston Avenue. Turn left (south) and walk until you see the **McBirney Estate** on your right. Pass through the gates to the front (south) in order to view the home, now part of the Rader Institute and Tulsa Regional Medical Center. Horatio Alger's innumerable books about a poor but worthy hero who enters life as a bootblack or newsboy and surmounts impossible obstacles to achieve the height of success finds a true life counterpart in the first owner of this mansion, James H. McBirney. James McBirney's wife was sister to Lee Clinton, and his daughter, an aviatress, a friend of Amelia Earhart.

McBirney selected the area along the Arkansas River for residential development, and retained a three-acre tract for himself. Many years later, the home was the first in Tulsa to be listed in the National Register of Historic Places. The asymmetrical design of the brick home, with its limestone trim and half timbering-stucco accents, comes together just as John Long, the architect intended—producing an incredibly grand home, but lacking the stiffness and formality usually associated with estates of this size. Appropriately described as Jacobethan architecture, a term compounded from Jacobean and Elizabethan, the home is an American equivalent of the English country manor. The off-center front door surrounded by a Tudor arched portal is lovely, as are the projecting gambrels and bays with their windows of leaded glass. The greatest difficulty with these brand-new mansions was to keep them from looking new. The home, in accordance with the architectural style, was intentionally rusticated, probably looking very much today as it did in 1927. The slate-floored terrace provides a beautiful view of the Arkansas River and the sloping grounds, which at one time encompassed a three-hole golf course.

JAMES MCBIRNEY: Baseball to Banking

Born in Ireland, James McBirney immigrated to the United States in 1875. Previously a janitor, McBirney began his career as a bookkeeper in Columbus, Kansas, later moving to Coffeyville where he worked for the Condon Commercial Bank. His prowess as a baseball pitcher brought him to the attention of the Tulsa Banking Company, which persuaded him to move to Tulsa. His success is legend from then on. In 1904 he was named a vice-president of the Tulsa Banking Company; one year later he and his brother Sam (a baseball coach for the University of Tulsa) began the Bank of Commerce, eventually the National Bank of Commerce.

McBirney Estate

Spotlight Theater

The pools below, stocked with rainbow trout by McBirney, give this site its original historical importance. Fed by an underground spring, they were known as one of Tulsa's famous "watering holes" where neighbors came to fill their pails with the cool, sweet water that was abundant. Earlier, the area had been a resting place for Indians, frontiersmen, and settlers who sat around camp fires, watered their stock, and replenished their flasks before fording the salty Arkansas. (The ferry later replaced the importance of this natural shale ford.) According to Tulsa lore, these springs also enjoyed the presence, in 1832, of Washington Irving, who was so impressed by the beauty here that he wrote about it.

Follow the driveway to the back of the house where you turn left onto Houston Avenue. Continue to Riverside Drive and cross for a good view of the Spotlight Theatre. Originally a music studio and recital hall, the home doubled as a residence for the instructor. A Bruce Goff design (Downtown Walk II) of 1929, the structure is art deco. The rigid cubism is reinforced by an enormous round window and other geometric shapes to create a modernity of form. Today it is a theatre hosting the performance of an old fashioned melodrama, *The Drunkard.* Your ticket includes the play, an olio afterwards consisting of vaudeville-type entertainment, and coffee and sandwiches. (The latter is considered by the troupe to be the last free lunch in town.) The play, performed every Saturday night, has been at this location for over four decades. For reservations call 587-5030.

Continue south on the bike path to your car. Think back to the Indians who loved the sandy river. "The mountains and hills, that you see, are your backbone, and the gullies and creeks, which are between the hills and mountains, are your heart veins!"

Downtown

ARRIVING IN TULSA FOR THE FIRST TIME on a hot summer day in August of 1920, Jenkin Lloyd Jones described his first impressions. "Here was a sprawling town of 75,000 newcomers baking in 105-degree heat. There weren't any trees except little sticks people had hopefully stuck out in their yards. The only water, besides an evil-smelling river, was a little mudhole called Orcutt Lake out at the end of the east side streetcar line."

Prices were "outrageous" because the young oiltown was booming, and "half the streets weren't paved." A typical Saturday night included a "testy mass of ranch hands, Indians and roustabouts that would gather at First and Main," and down the streets at the imported opera production "some of the oil queens clattered down the aisles looking like just-opened chests."

Fortunately, Tulsa grew quickly during the next seventy-five years, both in culture and in beauty. Today, the downtown area, the core of Tulsa's business community, offers a variety of cultural events and a pleasant setting for its many beautiful buildings and artworks.

The first downtown walk highlights many of the elegant older buildings that were built during the oil boom years. The second walk features some of Tulsa's most beautiful churches. Intersecting on the Main Mall, both walks include Bartlett Square, the landscaped fountain area, where places to eat are nearby.

WALK I

DISTANCE

1.5 miles

TIME

2 hours

WALK II

DISTANCE

1.5 miles

TIME

1.5 hours

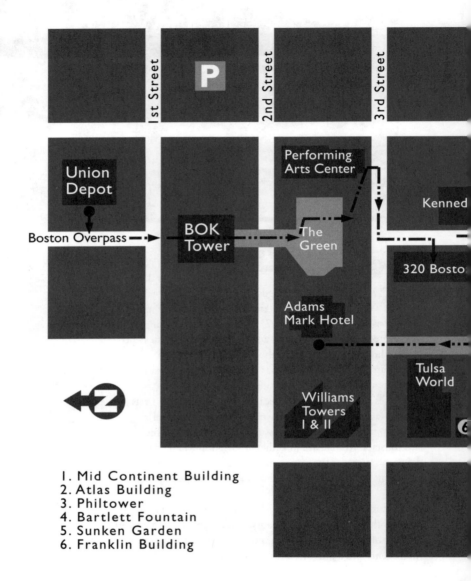

1st Street
2nd Street
3rd Street

P

Union Depot

Boston Overpass ▪▶

BOK Tower

Performing Arts Center

The Green

Kenned

320 Bosto

Adams Mark Hotel

Tulsa World

Williams Towers I & II

←**Z**

1. Mid Continent Building
2. Atlas Building
3. Philtower
4. Bartlett Fountain
5. Sunken Garden
6. Franklin Building

D O W N T O W N   I

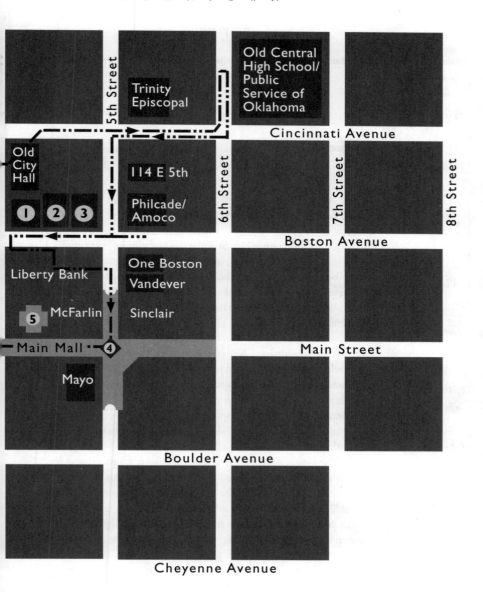

W A L K I

Winged wheel at
the Union Depot

*The desire for
machine-like,
geometric clarity
of the 1930s is
evident in the
Union Depot.
Chevrons,
sunbursts, eagles,
and winged
wheels symbolize
the future by
suggesting hope
and great
technical
advances in
travel.*

The most convenient place to park for the first walk is at a two-hour metered parking spot on a street close to the Bank of Oklahoma Tower between First and Second Streets.

THE UNION DEPOT. Walk to First Street between Cincinnati and Boston to view **The Union Depot,** a scene of parades and festivities on May 12, 1931, when a massive crowd of about 60,000 people (nearly half of Tulsa's population at that time) watched the opening. Tulsa's new "important front door" exhibited in its streamlined design symbols of hope for economic revival from the devastating Depression. Art deco in style, the building reflects the popular compulsion toward the aesthetics of machinery for inspiration. The desire for machine-like, geometric clarity evident in this building became something of a mania in the thirties. Chevrons, sunbursts, eagles, and winged wheels present on the exterior of the the building symbolize the future by suggesting hope and great technical advances in travel. Although in art deco the future was emphasized in theory, American architects tended to look for motifs in their own past, in the arts of the Mayans and of the Native Americans of the Southwest.

The Depot, servicing as many as thirty-six trains a day at its zenith, finally closed in 1967 from decreased rail travel. After fourteen years of neglect, the building shell was restored, and the inside, retaining art deco qualities, was adapted for office use. The entry lanterns, replicas of art deco fixtures, originally hung from the archway wall of the west entrance, and the new glass door with its zigzag handles preserves the boldness of design that was the hallmark of the art deco style. Such creative "recycling" of historically significant structures is part of a nationwide trend toward preservation. At its reopening in 1983, one national preservation expert remarked, "The Tulsa Union Depot is the most significant art deco renovation being done in the United States today."

Enter the lobby through the south entrance under the original archway, once the drive-in entrance for luggage removal. Take the elevator to the third floor balcony. Notice how the art deco interior and scale of space have been ingeniously preserved and integrated into office space. The vibrant colors of empress green, coral sand, and shades of grey in the ornamental plaster moldings and medallions on the ceiling are the restored original colors; the brandied crimson used throughout the building was selected to enhance the various shades of grey. The original bas-relief cartouches (ornamental panels) and the marble pilasters, eight feet above the floor, are also original to the Depot. The restoration along with the inclusion of such details as the streamlined handrails indicate the care taken to preserve the character and quality of the building.

BOSTON STREET OVERPASS. After retracing your steps through the south doors, walk north on the **Boston Street Overpass** to the Depot's west entrance. To your immediate north is the original commercial site of Tulsa. The railroad tracks below played a vital role in Tulsa's growth into a city. Not until the extension of the railroad line from Vinita to Tulsa in 1882 could Tulsa begin its dramatic growth. The railroad tracks also determined the skewed angle of downtown Tulsa in that Main Street was laid at a right angle to the tracks, which came in from the northeast.

BANK OF OKLAHOMA TOWER. Retrace your steps to the overpass to view the **Bank of Oklahoma Tower.** You now have an excellent view of Oklahoma's tallest office building, designed by Minoru Yamasaki, one of this country's most distinguished architects and designer of New York City's World Trade Center. The arched windows on the ground floor (visible from the front) temper the box-like severity of the structure. Wolf Von Echardt, noted architectural critic, commented that the Tower is "much better than the World Trade Center, the scale and the way it stands there." The 52-story building is part of the $300 million, nine-square block Williams Center (Yamasaki designed the master plan), generally acknowledged to have been the anchoring project for the subsequent flourishing of commercial construction on the north side of downtown. Located

DOWNTOWN EVENTS

MAYFEST: Usually the third week in May

CHILI/BLUEGRASS FESTIVAL: The first weekend after Labor Day

FIESTA: September

TULSA RUN: Last Saturday in October

CHRISTMAS PARADE OF LIGHTS: Usually the second Saturday in December.

ENTERTAINMENT: Most Tuesdays at noon at Bartlett Square, April through October.

PAC BROWN BAG IT MUSIC SERIES: Wednesdays at 12:10 in fall and spring.

For more information on these and other events, call: Downtown Tulsa Unlimited, 583-2617. Tulsa Performing Arts Center, 596-7105 (Brown Bag It Series) or 596-7122 (John Couey) to schedule a free backstage tour.

on the site of some of Tulsa's first buildings, this development, including a hotel, performing arts center, five office buildings, the Depot, and a green area, is recognized nationally as an outstanding urban project.

Enter the Tower from the north; take the escalators to the second floor. Before exiting to the pedestrian bridge, notice the stainless steel sculpture. The two-and-one-half-ton piece by St. Louis artists William Severson and Saunders Schultz represents the Bank of Oklahoma logo, a hexagonal shape of interconnecting Os.

THE GREEN. Walk outside on the bridge to the **Green**, a two-and-one-half acre park built on top of a parking garage. Besides the many beautiful displays of seasonal plantings and a waterfall, the Green is the home of the bronze sculpture by Tulsa artist Jay O'Meilia. The ballerina symbolizes *The Four Moons,* Tulsa Ballet Theater's ballet honoring Oklahoma's internationally known Indian ballerinas.

Continue south through the Green and turn left (east) on the main walk. In the sidewalk locate the aluminum plaque, indicating the site of the first service of Trinity Episcopal Church.

Williams Center Green
looking west

PERFORMING ARTS CENTER. Two more pieces of sculpture are located near the **Performing Arts Center.** The first piece, at the top of the stairs, is *Seaform* by Barbara Hepworth, an internationally recognized British artist who worked with Henry Moore and Ben Nicholson. Descend the stairs to view the untitled piece by David Lee Brown, who studied at the prestigious Cranbrook Academy of Art. The spiraling shape creates wonderful reflections of light.

Continue to the Third Street entrance of the Performing Arts Center. Inside the lobby is New York artist Stan Landsman's glass and stainless steel structure. Forty-one stainless steel wires, each supporting fifty pounds, suspend this work from the ceiling. The reflections of the piece are mirrored in the wall above. (The enormous task of cleaning the sculpture goes up for bidding twice a year.) Throughout the building are over fifty pieces of art including works by nationally recognized local artists, such as the late Alexander Hogue and P. S. Gordon, and other famous artists such as Louise Nevelson.

After you leave the Performing Arts Center, look at the mural, *Banner Walls,* across the street. Local artist, the late Jim Corlett, used brightly colored banners to give both a renaissance and contemporary feeling to the area.

320 BOSTON BUILDING. Retrace your steps to the light and cross to the **320 Boston Building.** This massive stone and brick building has housed banks, including the Exchange National Bank, since its opening in 1917. In 1923, a twelve-floor addition was added to the south side of the original twelve-story building. Four years later a tower was added, making it Tulsa's tallest building. It rose 57-feet above the Philtower, which had been Tulsa's skyscraper for only a few months. These two buildings continued to dominate Tulsa's skyline for the next thirty years until the 32-story Fourth National Bank Building was completed in 1957 at Sixth Street and Boulder Avenue.

Before you enter the lobby off Boston Avenue, look at the intricate carvings on the monumental brass doors and the elaborate ornamentation of floral motifs carved in the stone archway. Inside the lobby is a ceiling decoration painted on canvas that was recently uncovered and restored. The style is loosely Greek

Barbara Hepworth's *Seaform*

Hepworth first introduced into England the use of the "hole." Adopted by Moore in 1932, the "hole" was crucial to Moore and Hepworth in their innovations in sculptural form. Suggesting some deep-sea crustacean or coral growth, *Seaform* reflects Hepworth's emotional identification with nature.

S. G. KENNEDY

Kennedy, a pioneer physician in 1891 when Tulsa was a frontier village of only 150 people, originally built his first home on this site. Then after ten years, Kennedy moved to North Osage Drive, on the Osage reservation, to take advantage of his wife's Indian allotment. Kennedy later became involved in the development of petroleum fields in Oklahoma and in property investments after retiring from his medical practice in 1907. He acquired and helped develop the Kennedy and Springer Oil Lease of 4,780 acres, which was the greatest production well in the Osage Nation and was pumping 10,000 barrels of oil daily when it sold for $12.5 million in 1916. In 1917 Kennedy purchased the Gallais Building on his old homesite and added this second unit facing Boston Avenue two years later.

and Roman; the motifs are purely decorative and fanciful. The lobby retains the original marble flooring, polished brass elevator doors, and highly detailed moldings. Contrasting in style are the curved, sleek escalators reminiscent of the thirties.

KENNEDY BUILDING. An interesting route to take to the **Kennedy Building** across the street is the tunnel. Take the escalator down to a short flight of stairs behind the escalators. Turn left and enter the tunnel under the plexiglass sign marked "Tunnel to Autoramp." First, you will enter a green tunnel and then pass through a tiled and multicolored tunnel. Enter the double doors on your left, marked "The Kennedy Building," and take the stairs to the ten-story atrium, which highlights the renovation of the building.

The atrium provides a dramatic, open, light-filled space and encloses offices whose windows originally opened to the outside. (For a spectacular view, take the elevator to the top floor and look down.) New corridors were added to the exterior of the atrium to make the interior office space more usable. During renovation, the original brass elevator doors were restored and turned to face the atrium. Nearby is one of J. Seward Johnson's bronze sculptures (Swan Lake Walk). Take time to see what he is reading.

You are now standing in the second addition to the Kennedy Building. The original part, erected in 1915 by S. Gallais, a St. Louis real estate developer and early investor in Tulsa, was to the south. Gallais bought the land from Dr. S. G. Kennedy. Enter the lobby behind the elevator doors, where you will see the original Italian and Vermont marble floors and walls. Much care was used in cutting and applying the marble blocks on the walls to produce a decorative pattern. Greek moldings of egg and dart motif encircle the room under the plaster-coffered ceiling.

After you exit onto Boston Avenue, turn your attention to the lion-headed gargoyles above the doors. They once held rings in their mouths to support the original canopy. You now have an excellent view of the 320 Boston Building across the street. Notice the arches, moldings, and lion heads, adjacent to the second floor windows.

Turn left (south) and walk toward the clock on the Mid-Continent Building. At the corner turn left and walk east. As you pass the Fourth Street entrance to the Kennedy Building, find "Gallais" carved in stone over the doorway.

Egg and dart molding, Kennedy Building

TULSA MUNICIPAL BUILDING. Before you cross Fourth Street, you have a good view of the **Tulsa Municipal Building,** the old city hall. Enter the Fourth Street lobby and look at the mural completed during the 1975 remodeling. Painted by Delbert Jackson (his self portrait is in the model T Ford), it depicts a Tulsa street scene from 1919. Notice the trolley with Orcutt Lake (Swan Lake Walk) written on its side. This was the end of the line at that time.

TRINITY EPISCOPAL CHURCH. Walk through the Municipal Building to the Cincinnati Avenue exit; turn right (south) and cross Fifth Street to view **Trinity Episcopal Church.** Trinity Church has been located on this corner since 1906, when the site was previously an apple orchard. This structure is a fine example of Late English Gothic Revival architecture, a movement that took up the English Gothic where it had stopped during the reign of Henry VIII and carried the movement forward to mesh with the late nineteenth and early twentieth century architect's own creative philosophy. The church, started in 1920 and finished six years later, was designed by Bertram Grovesnor Goodhue, a pacesetter of this movement from New York City, with Tulsa George Winkler assisting. According to former Rector Dr. Edward Eckel, "Trinity is the best example of true Gothic architecture between St. Louis and the West Coast." The detailing and proportions emphasize its verticality (an element of the Gothic style) and contribute to Trinity's architectural success. Two life-size marble sculptures, made in Italy and installed in the 1960s, flank the main entrance. On the left is Moses, the law-giver; on the right is Elijah, the prophet of monotheism. The water from the rock and cruse of oil at their feet have a special relevance to eastern Oklahoma.

Enter the **garden courtyard** from Cincinnati Avenue. On the arched entrance notice the small sculpture of St. Fiacre,

TULSA MUNICIPAL BUILDING

Classified as neoclassic, the building recalls many elements of Greek and Roman styles, including box-like form, symmetry and balance, clear demarcation of levels, and applied Ionic half-columns. Designed by the Rush, Endacott and Rush architectural firm and built in 1919, the building was remodeled in 1975. It was the first building to be adapted for contemporary office use.

DOWNTOWN CHURCHES

Trinity Episcopal Church (582-4128) sells lunches Tuesday and Thursday at noon and offers 30-minute organ recitals on Tuesday at 12:05 from October to May. Open weekdays 8:30 to 4:30, Saturday 8:30 to 1:00, and Sunday 7:00 to 1:00.

First Church of Christ is locked; to see the interior, call 583-8923 Monday through Thursday between 9:00 and noon.

Holy Family Cathedral is usually locked. Visit during Masses Saturdays 3:00 p.m. to 6:00 p.m. and Sundays 7:00 a.m. to 6:00 p.m., or call 582-6247 for a tour.

First Christian Church is open weekdays 8:00 to 4:30, Saturdays 9:00 to noon, Sundays 8:00 to noon and 4:40 to 8:00 p.m. (The entrances on Boulder Avenue are usually locked; entrances are in the back off Main Street.)

First Methodist Church is open weekdays 8:30 to 5:00 and Sundays from 8:30 to 1:00.

Boston Avenue Methodist Church is open weekdays 9:00 to 5:00. Enter through the south entrance. Volunteers are usually available to answer questions about the church. Thirty to 45-minute tours start in the library on Sundays at noon, or call 583-5181 to arrange a tour.

patron saint of gardens. The enclosed garden is a relief from the urban setting and provides a European flavor. To enter the church, proceed to the door at the end of the garden. The sanctuary is to the left. Start your tour of the church in the narthex, the western foyer, and look down the center aisle. The church, with its cruciform plan, is typical of Gothic architecture with the entrance from the west and the altar in the east.

The **stained glass windows in the clerestory** (upper sections), remarkable expressions of Biblical salvation, Oklahoma history, and twentieth-century world history, owe their iconographical selection to the Reverend C. W. V. Junker, Trinity's Rector Emeritus, and to Frederick Cole of Canterbury, England. Cole, a world-class stained glass expert who restored the twelfth-century stained glass windows of Canterbury Cathedral (mother church of all Anglicans), created the windows. At first glance the windows appear traditional, but upon closer inspection, many contemporary references are evident. On the last two panels on the southwest corner are the faces of Hitler, Mussolini, Goering, and Goebbels in the smoky blue panes of glass. These men represent the anti-Christs of our time in history; other Bosch-like distortions depict the Seven Deadly Sins: pride, covetousness, lust, anger, gluttony, envy, and sloth. The twenty panels on both the north and south sides of the clerestory sections represent Articles of Faith as contained

Trinity Episcopal Church

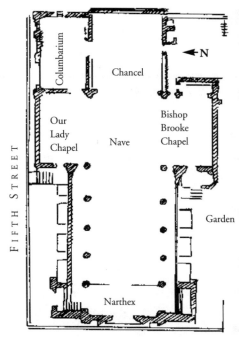

Chancel

Columbarium

Our Lady Chapel

Nave

Bishop Brooke Chapel

← N

Garden

Narthex

FIFTH STREET

Trinity Church.

in the Apostles' Creed—from the Annunciation to the Resurrection. To read the panels, start on the south side and read from left to right around to the north side. Original to the church are the **lower stained glass windows**, which tell of the miracles of Christ (the south side) and the parables (the north side). The **Four Great Windows** relate to the Apostles' Creed. Begin reading at the east window over the altar and end at the north window.

In the **Bishop Brooke Chapel** (south transept) notice the finely detailed needlepoint kneelers, made by the women and friends of Trinity, of historically significant places in Tulsa and Oklahoma. The three long kneeling cushions in the altar area include a depiction of the original Trinity Church and a 1980 modern scene of Tulsa. The church scene has 85,000 stitches and took over 450 hours to complete. Other individual kneelers include Boston Avenue Church, Council Oak Tree, Swan Lake, and Philbrook.

Continuing to the **chancel** area, notice the **reredos** (carved wooden backdrop) behind the high altar of Carrara marble. (Michelangelo used this highly desired marble for his sculptures.) In the center of the reredos is Christ the King with His scepter and orb. Flanking Him are representatives of the various strains of Christianity. From left to right are: St. Patrick/Irish, St Augustine/Roman, St. Athanasius/Greek, and Thomas a Becket/British. The figures were carved by Anton Lang of Oberammergau, Germany, scene of the famous passion play. On the ceiling are paintings, by the late Tulsa artist Delbert Jackson, depicting symbols related to the crucifixion of Jesus. Beginning at the northwest are the thirty pieces of silver, and on the southwest are Judas and Pontius Pilate. The pipe organ is acknowledged to be one of the ten finest church organs in America. It has 4,431 pipes, ranging in size from six inches to over thirty-two feet.

At first glance the windows appear traditional, but upon closer inspection, many contemporary references are evident. . . . Hitler, Mussolini, Goering, and Goebbels in the smoky blue panes of glass.

TRINITY'S MADONNA AND CHILD

Josephena de Vasconcellos created Trinity's statue of the Madonna and Child, the centerpiece of the Chapel of Our Lady. Vasconcellos's works are included in St. Paul's Cathedral and other leading churches in England; she is also the designer of the Christmas creche in London's Trafalgar Square. Originally in the Chapel Royal at Windsor Castle, the statue was sent to the crypt of the bombed Coventry Cathedral as an "earnest" that Coventry would be rebuilt by donations from all over the world. Later, the statue arrived at Trinity on Christmas of 1958. The little lamb and turtle doves represent offerings that were taken to the temple soon after a child's birth during Biblical times. This Child's unusual position refers to His being offered to the world as the "Lamb of God."

In **The Chapel of Our Lady** (north transept) is the original 1908 altar of the first Trinity Church. The chapel also houses a statue of the Madonna and Child, sculpted by England's leading sculptress, Josephena de Vasconcellos. Needlepoint kneelers tell the story of Mary's life.

To visit the **Chapel of the Good Shepherd**, (the Crypt) known as the Columbarium, which houses the ashes of deceased members and friends of Trinity, proceed through the east doorway and turn left at the first door. Descend the stairs to the statue, a reproduction of one of the oldest (third-century) three-dimensional carvings of Jesus. The original statue stood in the entryway to the catacombs. The marble reproduction, crafted in Florence, Italy, is one of the very few in the world. Enter the room to your left. On the north wall is *The Supper of the Lord,* a stained-glass window fashioned by Cole. The unusual translation of the Last Supper features the table in the shape of a fish, the symbol of abundant life. Here Christ wears purple instead of the traditional white and a workman's crown instead of the halo. The elongated, stylized faces of the group seem to be Byzantine-inspired. Under the window, notice the vibrant colors of the needlepoint cushions that duplicate those in the window.

Old Central. After leaving Trinity, turn left and continue south to the corner of Sixth Street and Cincinnati Avenue. On the southeast corner stands the renovated Old Central High School, presently the headquarters of Public Service Company of Oklahoma. In 1916, when the cornerstone was laid, businesses closed and thousands of people turned out for the dedication. Walk to the north side of the building on Sixth Street to see dated stones representing each graduating class; above the entrance is the year 1916. On either side of the entrance are two medallions with an oil lamp resting on three books, symbols of knowledge. Gothic influences are indicated by the arched entrance, the crenelations (square indentations) over the doorway, the foliage motifs, and the coats of arms. The symmetry of the building is a renaissance conception classifying the structure as a version of the English Renaissance.

114 EAST FIFTH STREET. Retrace your steps north to Fifth Street and turn left (west). On the south side is a charming, small building built in 1926, designed by John Duncan Forsythe a prominent Tulsa architect who designed Southern Hills Country Club. His building at 114 East Fifth Street shows Georgian influences in the symmetry and proportion of the building, the contrast of the white trim against the red brick, and a psuedo-Palladian window with a panel to suggest a fanlight.

AMOCO NORTH. Next door to the west is **Amoco North,** previously the Philcade, built by Waite Phillips, one of Tulsa's most generous philanthropists (Philbrook Museum of Art Walk). On entering the exceedingly ornate lobby (in the shape of a "T" for Tulsa), you will be amazed at the amount of rich detail. Expensive materials of gilt, bronze, and marble are everywhere. Evidences of art deco appear in the zigzag motifs of the light fixtures and in the grill work over the north window. Chevrons and geometric designs abound on the walls and ceilings. The swirling lines of the foliage motif derived from Art Nouveau provide contrast to the extensive use of metals used in the archways and the metallic gold shimmer surrounding the chandeliers. The elaborate, rich surface is a feast for the eyes, symbolizing nothing but pure enjoyment.

Exit the Philcade onto Boston Avenue and spend some time viewing the exterior. For a better view, cross the street. The facade is a mixture of terra

OLD CENTRAL

At its closing in 1976, more than 44,000 students had received their diplomas from Central High School. The north half of the school, designed by George Winkler, was completed during the summer of 1917 at a cost of $380,855. The south half was added in 1922, making the building the second largest high school in the nation.

Detail (above left) and north entrance, Old Central High School

Waite Phillips's initials in the Amoco North/Philcade Building.

The Philcade was Phillips's response to future downtown development toward Boulder Avenue and away from Boston Avenue, the location of his Philtower building. He reacted to the potential threat by erecting a nine-story building the same color as the Philtower but with a plainer facade so as not to compete with the Philtower's tenants.

cotta, brick, and metalwork designs. Notice the "WP" on the top of the building and over all the doors. The profusion of motifs includes various birds, reptiles, and mammals hidden in the stylized foliage above the ground floor windows. The building was completed in 1930, but within a short time an additional four stories were added.

PHILTOWER. Across Fifth Street is **The Philtower,** a reminder of the glitter and wealth prevalent during Tulsa's oil boom years and once the "queen of the Tulsa skyline." During 1927, the year of its completion, "more than a million dollars a month was spent on downtown building. Tulsans at this time erected skyscrapers not so much because ground space was at a premium, but because they liked to see them rise" (Angie Debo). Height was such a source of delight to the owners that they took great pride in outdoing each other, a pride indicated by the taller tower built at 320 Boston soon after the Philtower's completion. The elaborate facade of the Philtower is rich in detail featuring gargoyles and the initials of Waite Phillips over the Boston Avenue entrance, a twenty-five foot arch. The polychromed tile roof, predominantly red and green, is still a skyline landmark. Designed by Edward Buehler Delk of Kansas City (he also designed Villa Philbrook), the Philtower reflects late English Gothic influences on both the exterior and the interior.

Enter the lobby from Boston Avenue through the reinstalled brass doors. (In the 1980s these and the doors on Fifth Street were found at the Camelot Inn and returned.) The sculptured ceiling with fan-vaulted tracery was fashioned in Italy. It is reported that it took two years to construct the ceiling. Other Gothic motifs include the stair railings and the arched doorways. The floors and walls are travertine marble; the chandeliers were designed for the building. Massive elevator doors, handsomely framed in marble, are of brass and feature the distinctive "WP" shield in their upper panels. Waite Phillips's initials are found throughout the building on brass knobs (one is in the lobby next to the Boston entrance).

In 1941 Phillips donated the Philtower to the Boy Scouts of America to endow the Philmont Boy Scout Ranch, in New

Mexico, which he had given earlier. The Scouts sold the building in 1977.

MID-CONTINENT BUILDING. After leaving the Philtower, turn right and continue north on Boston Avenue to the **Mid-Continent Building,** formerly the Cosden Building. During 1917-18 Josh Cosden (Riverview Walk), the "prince of petroleum" built Tulsa's first real "skyscraper"—sixteen stories—on the site of the old 1884 Mission, Tulsa's first school. Costing $1,000,000, the building was one of the world's tallest concrete structures at that time. The Mid-Continent Building is Sullivanesque architecture, recognized by its intricate weaving of linear and geometric forms and stylized foliage in the symmetrical pattern. Louis Sullivan (1856 - 1924), an historically significant American architect, was one of the few persons to whom Frank Lloyd Wright publicly acknowledged a debt of influence in his career. In 1980 the former owners, Reading and Bates, renovated and added a 36-story addition to the east and twenty floors cantilevered over the original structure. This unusual structural solution was necessary because the original footing of the building could not support a tall addition. The facade of the building is a Venetian Gothic terra cotta veneer, replicated on the new additions.

Walk under the cast-iron canopy to the Boston Avenue lobby. Only the lobby retains its original appearance with its lavish ornamentation and its Georgian marble walls and floors. The great care taken in choice of marbles is illustrated by the contrast between the black and white marbled walls and the black stairs. Byzantine inspired Venetian details embellish the terra cotta band that encircles the room and caps and unifies the space. The chandelier repeats the same theme of lushness.

Go up the stairs to view the drilling rig sculpture by Jay O'Meilia and then down stairs to the right to enter the new lobby. On the east side is a marvelous stained-glass representation by Tulsa artist Ciccy McCaa of Tulsa's skyline when the tower was completed in 1984. Take the escalators or elevator downstairs to find six large photographs taken in Tulsa between 1896 and 1931 that give you a good idea of the city's growth during that time.

JOSH CODEN: Prince of Petroleum

Josh Cosden was "a lightning rod for triumphs and tragedies." In 1909 a cyclone leveled his first Oklahoma refining plant and a fire destroyed the rebuilt plant. From the debris of these calamities, Cosden built the world's largest independent refinery by 1913. At 39, Cosden was worth over $50,000,000. After a scandalous divorce and remarriage, Cosden and his bride left an unforgiving Tulsa society for New York's elite "Four Hundred." "Game Josh, rubberball of the oil industry" lost and regained his fortunes several times. During the Depression he lost his fortune in the cotton market in New Orleans. Poor health prevented his comeback and in 1940 his company went into receivership and his private property was sold at public auction. Cosden, 59, died four days later of a heart attack.

A lion holding a shield, the McFarlin Building

ATLAS LIFE BUILDING. Retrace your steps to the Boston exit, cross Boston Avenue at Fourth Street, and walk toward **First Place Tower.** Look back across the street for the monumental Atlas holding the world perched on the roof edge of the **Atlas Life Building.** Built in 1922, the building is in the shape of an inverted "T," a shape which provided natural ventilation and light. The architects, Rush, Endacott and Rush, designed several other buildings downtown, including the Municipal Building that you saw earlier.

FIRST PLACE TOWER. First National Bank opened on October 5, 1973 in what was the tallest building in Tulsa until the Bank of Oklahoma opened four years later. Before entering the lobby, inspect the remains, located near the Boston Avenue's south entrance, of the old bank. Inside is a brass sculpture of Icarus, the Greek mythological character who fell into the sea when the sun melted the wax on his wings. Walk south through the lobby to the escalator and ascend to Liberty Bank's lobby. On the west wall behind the tellers is a mural, by Fred W. Conway of St. Louis, depicting the Oklahoma Territory land run.

ONE BOSTON PLAZA. Exit the bank onto Fifth Street. Directly across the brick mall is **One Boston Plaza,** formerly the Thompson Building, another example of Sullivanesque. Built in 1923, the building was originally only as tall as the lighter colored limestone band on the building's mid-section. Later, five floors and the illuminated copper and limestone dome were added.

To your right (west) is **Bartlett Square Fountain.** The fountain area is an excellent example of a good use of public space. Situated on the Main Mall at a major crossroads, it is near food services and accessible from different directions. The irregular design of the fountain is an interesting piece of sculpture providing a variety of places to sit and to enjoy the beauty of trees and flowers. The sounds of water along with its movement and manipulation of light add a delightful foil to the static backdrop of the high-rise buildings. Take a rest and experience what most downtowners do—eating, people watching, or enjoying noon-time entertainment. While resting, you can view two more buildings adjacent to the fountain area — **The Sinclair Building** and the **McFarlin Building.** Interesting classical molding details of the McFarlin building include the key fret, egg and dart, and bead and reel motifs. Other ornamentations include crests with the fleur-de-lis, lions, and pilasters.

NORTH ON MAIN MALL. From here, continue your walk north along Main Mall. Now you have a good view of the **Exchange Tower,** 320 Boston Building, which resembles a temple facade. When the tower was illuminated in 1938, people twenty miles away reported seeing it. For thirty years, the Exchange Tower, the Philtower, and the Thompson Building formed Tulsa's skyline. They were called the "three musketeers."

When you are parallel with the back of the First Place Tower, look back at Jim Corlett's grey and white mural, *Trees,* completed in 1978. Immediately north of *Trees* is the **First Place Plaza Sunken Garden.** Look down over the railings at the graceful, welded bronze fountain, designed by world-famous sculptor, Harry Bertoia of Philadelphia, Pennsylvania. To the east, just north of the First Place Tower, is another sculpture, constructed of black fiberglass. The artist, Gottfried Honegger, a native of Zurich, Switzerland, designed the spheres in his Paris studio. He has received international acclaim for his one-man shows in London, Paris, and New York. The piece is thirteen and one-half feet tall, large enough for people to walk through. Honegger is noted for his unique treatment of

Atlas holding the world, Atlas Life Building

SINCLAIR, MCFARLIN, AND THE EXCHANGE BANK

On the Sinclair Building's roofline is a cartouche with a carved "S," signifying that this building was built by oilman Harry Sinclair. Another oilman and friend of Sinclair's, Robert H. McFarlin (Riverview Walk) built a building in 1918 on the northeast corner. McFarlin and Sinclair joined forces to help organize the Exchange National Bank of Tulsa in 1910. The bank was financed by 30 of Tulsa's wealthiest independent oil producers, thereby preventing a Rockefeller and Mellon monopoly in the petroleum industry. The policies of the bank were one of the major reasons that Tulsa became the oil capital of the world.

Notice the shapes reflected in the dark glass of the two Williams Towers and the spatial relationships created between the buildings when viewed from different angles. The corners of the polygon-shaped structures create unique office spaces.

spheres which emphasize the importance of form in space.

Continue north on the Main Mall to Third Street. Notice the shapes reflected in the dark glass of the two Williams Towers and the spatial relationships created between the buildings when viewed from different angles. The corners of the polygon-shaped structures create unique office spaces. Originally on this site stood the Kress Building, demolished in 1972. Because Samuel Kress built one of his many retail stores in Tulsa, in 1931, Tulsa became one of the few cities to receive the important Kress collection of Renaissance and Baroque works (Philbrook Museum of Art Walk).

You can return to your car a few blocks away by walking through the Adam's Mark Hotel or the Green area and BOK Tower.

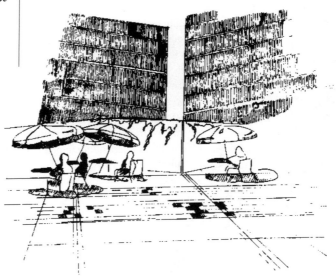

Plaza between William Towers
and the Adam's Mark Hotel

W A L K   I I

The best place to park for this walk is either the First Methodist Church parking lot on the southwest corner of Eleventh Street and Boulder Avenue or behind the First Christian Church at Tenth and Main Streets.

FIRST CHURCH OF CHRIST, SCIENTIST. The walk begins in front of **First Church of Christ, Scientist** on the northwest corner of Tenth Street and Boulder Avenue. Christian Science services have been held in Tulsa since 1900, but the building was not completed until April 1, 1923. The basic design is a Greek cross, originated in Byzantine times. It utilizes a square floor plan with a circular dome and vaulted ceilings. The dome rests on pendentives—four concave spherical triangles of masonry rising from the square corners and bending inward to form a circular base for the dome. The pendentives make the transition from the square ground floor to the dome above. (In 532, Emperor Justinian's engineers and architects from Asia Minor used the pendentive method when building Hagia Sophia in Constantinople.) From ancient times the dome has been viewed as an analogue of the dome in heaven, turning people's aspirations upward, admitting celestial light and glorifying God.

Classical elements on the exterior include the Roman-derived dome and the Greek Ionic Columns, numbering ten to symbolize the Commandments. The small lion heads, peering out of the honeysuckle border above the church's name, are symbols of grace and strength from the Renaissance. The Greek key fret design, encircling the dome in relief, signifies continuity of life.

In 1943, Dr. Adah Robinson remodeled and redecorated the inside of the church with a scheme that harmonized with the classical architecture on the exterior. Subsequent redecorations have retained Dr. Robinson's plan. Remarks written by Dr. Robinson about the interior and exterior are available by request.

In 532, Emperor Justinian's engineers and architects from Asia Minor used the pendentive method when building Hagia Sophia in Constantinople. From ancient times the dome has been viewed as an analogue of the dome in heaven, turning people's aspirations upward, admitting celestial light and glorifying God.

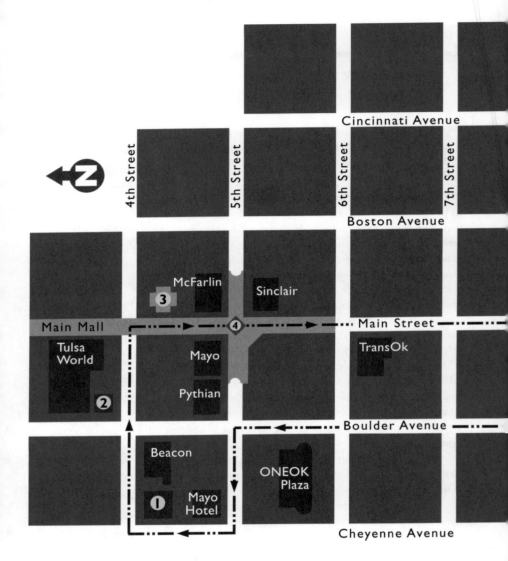

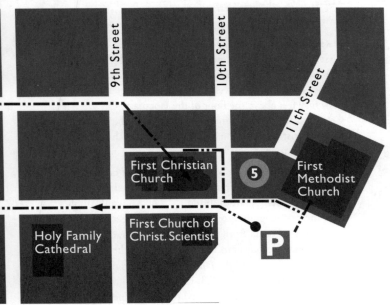

8th Street

1. Martindale
2. Franklin Building
3. Sunken Garden
4. Bartlett Fountain
5. Cathedral Square

9th Street

10th Street

11th Street

First Christian Church

5

First Methodist Church

Holy Family Cathedral

First Church of Christ. Scientist

P

DOWNTOWN II

First Christian
Church domes

FIRST CHRISTIAN CHURCH. Directly across the street is the **First Christian Church**, notable for its stained glass dome. An eclectic mixture of various styles—Byzantine, Baroque, and Rococo—the dome is twenty-six feet in diameter and rises more than fifty feet above the floor of the sanctuary. On top is a Celtic cross, patterned after one dating from the early centuries of the Christian era. (The interior of this church is included later in this tour.)

HOLY FAMILY. Begin walking toward **Holy Family Cathedral.** Notice the French Gothic spires juxtaposed against the stark, modern Transok Building. The Roman Catholics were the first religious group in Tulsa to create a permanent building. Dedicated April 1, 1914, the cathedral, housing one of the largest Gothic altars in the nation, was the largest church built in Oklahoma and the tallest building in Tulsa until the Mayo Hotel was built in 1923. Lighter, more graceful, and almost weightless when compared to its Romanesque predecessor, a Gothic-styled church was characterized by "reaching heavenward as prayer." Three vertical spires represent the Holy Family. The tallest spire is faced with four large clocks; the crosses on the spires are ten feet in height. Adorning the main entrance on Boulder Avenue is the Latin inscription meaning, "This is the House of God." There are 163 windows in the cathedral; most are stained glass and shaped in the style of the Gothic arch. Stained glass windows from the demolished original 1899 church are included in the Chapel of Peace. Brochures explaining the stained glass and interior are available on request.

ONEOK. After viewing the church, continue walking north on Boulder Avenue past the **Oneok Building** (pronounced one-oak.) Originally slated to have fifty-two stories, the building's projected height was pared to its current seventeen floors during the oil bust of the early 1980s.

Holy Family Cathedral spire

PYTHIAN BUILDING. A casualty of an earlier fluctuating economy is the **Pythian Building**, located on the northeast corner of Fifth Street and Boulder Avenue. Built in 1930 by two local oil men, J. M. Gillette and H. C. Tyrrell (Maple Ridge Walk I), the building was purchased the following year by the Knights of Phythias. The structure was originally intended to have a ten-story hotel on top of its current three stories, but the Depression not only cancelled the plans for the hotel but forced the original owners to sell the building soon after completion.

The facade is a mixture of cream and multi-colored terra cotta, glass in metal frames, marble insets, and granite. In 1930 the architect Edward W. Saunders described the building and decoration as faintly suggesting several types of architecture but "as a whole" being "distinctly modern." Strong vertical zigzag designs are expressed on the exterior walls broken by an unusual canopy over the Fifth Street entrance. Unfortunately the lobby is kept locked. Inside, alive with art deco features, the floor design is derived from Native American motifs. The multi-colored tiles, decorative plaster ceiling with beams and haunches, light fixtures, etched glass windows, grand stairway, and detailed cast-iron railing are all original. On the Boulder side of the Pythian Building, notice the metal marquee with its unusual light fixtures.

MANHATTAN BUILDING AND MAYO HOTEL. A stark contrast to the richly, elaborate Pythian Building is the renovated **Manhattan Building** across Boulder Avenue. It is one of three buildings on Fifth Street built by the Mayo family. The Mayo brothers, John and Cass, came to Tulsa in 1904 and opened a furniture store on Main Street. They became very successful and played an important role in Tulsa's early years. The Manhattan Building housed the Mayo Furniture business for over fifty years. Built in 1921, it is one of only a few remaining buildings from Tulsa's pre-art deco construction boom that still retains its original simple facade. Notice the cartouches, above the second and eighth stories, which soften the building's straightforward lines. A dentil cornice crowns the building.

Next door to the west is the once luxurious **Mayo Hotel**, designed by George Winkler and constructed in 1924 by the Mayo brothers. Once the tallest building in Oklahoma, the eighteen-story, six hundred-room hotel hosted such notables as Charlie Chaplin, Mae West, Charles Lindbergh, Bob Hope, several presidents and was for many years the home of oil magnate J. Paul Getty.

The Martindale, exhibiting a highly decorated terra cotta facade, is Tulsa's most ornate building. Each terra cotta piece was crafted through an extremely intricate and painstaking process.

MARTINDALE BUILDING. Turn right at Cheyenne Avenue and walk north to the **Martindale Building**, built as a hotel to capitalize on the 1928 International Petroleum Exposition. I. S. "Ike" Mincks constructed the hotel in 1927 at a cost of $800,000. He later had to liquidate in 1935, and the hotel acquired a new owner and name —the Adams.

Exhibiting a highly decorated terra cotta facade, this is Tulsa's most ornate building. Each terra cotta piece was crafted through an extremely intricate and painstaking process. The surface design, shrinkage, glazing, and firing were precisely controlled. The exterior pattern was divided into sections weighing up to several hundred pounds, making manageable units with structural integrity. The units were dried before firing, a process that took weeks at 1,000° F. or more and was controlled to assure proper shrinkage and to avoid cracking. (For an example of 1980s terra cotta, see the new addition on the Mid-Continent Building, Downtown Walk I.)

The Spanish facade combines exuberant decorations with imagination and flourish. The exterior is widely recognized as an excellent example of glazed terra cotta veneering. Notice the pastel blues and reds, and the intricately styled gargoyles, shields, and griffins. The "M" on the canopies is for the original owner, Mincks. Additional terra cotta craftsmanship can be seen inside the lobby.

EAST ON FOURTH STREET. Turn right (east) onto Fourth Street and walk toward Boulder Avenue. Across the street to your left is the new location for **Coney Island**, "a Tulsa tradition since 1926." Today, the hurried business people of downtown appreciate the fast service. Although the menu is limited, the quality of the food is good and the prices are low.

On the corner of Fourth and Boulder is the **Beacon Building,** built in 1923 by Waite Phillips (Philbrook Museum of Art Walk). Until 1976 the building had a beacon light tower, which symbolized the long-time tenant, the Beacon Life Insurance Company. It was removed because of problems with pigeons that favored the structure. Notice the cast-iron canopies, the gracefully arched windows, the pilasters, the moldings, and the shield on the exterior.

MAIN MALL. Continue walking east until you reach the **Main Mall.** Look diagonally across the street to the northeast corner of Fourth and Main Streets. The **Reunion Center** was designed by Rush, Endacott and Rush architectural firm in 1919 for the First National Bank. Six years later, the bank

A 5-CENT LUNCH

At a time when bathtub gin was the rage of Chicago and frenzied flappers danced the Charleston in big cities back East, the delicious, new 5-cent sandwich called the "coney island" was the rage in Tulsa. The founder, Christ Economou, had come to America in 1911 from Greece and worked his way west. Believing the young, growing Tulsa to be the ideal place to open a store, Economou chose to stay. The strange, new sandwich caught on quickly, and in 1946 Economou moved his restaurant nearby.

Main Mall looking south

LOCHAPOKA GAMES

The intersection of Sixth and Main Streets was once the playing field used by the Creek Indians for their ball games in the late 1800s. Regarded as "the brother of war," the games were prestigious displays of skill for the Indians. (Visit Philbrook Museum of Art to see Terry Saul's *Stickball Game*.) David O. Gillis, a Tulsan who watched the Lochapoka games in his boyhood, vividly described these exciting contests:

The players were painted with gay colors in grotesque designs over their bodies. The breechcloth, the only article of clothing, was surmounted by a belt hung with coon tails, the yellow rings on the black fur contrasting with the colors on the body. The speeches finished, the chief or chosen umpire tossed the ball. Then followed the mighty scramble. If the ball fell to the ground the players bunched in a huddle, a seething mass of humanity, to recover it. Their tails bobbing in the wind, snarls and yells emanating from the tangle, they resembled nothing so much as a pack of hungry animals fighting to death for flesh. Clubs clashed against each other or smashed on heads. Blood flowed and bodies were mauled this way or that. If a player was injured or killed, the play never stopped but the umpire dragged the victim out of bounds and left him under a tree till the game was finished. When a score was made the air resounded with gobbles, the age old challenge of the Indian, until one half expected to see men turned before his very eyes into a flock of turkeys. The onlookers not only liked the fight, but often bet heavily on the game, wagering their horses and cows.

—D. O. GILLIS

expanded the building to its present height of ten stories. Placed on the National Register of Historic Places and restored in 1979, the refurbished building reflects its 1925 appearance. Two-story stone arches, brick pilasters, and paired windows with stone spandrels provide the structure's vertical emphasis.

BARTLETT SQUARE. Turn right (south) and walk toward the **Bartlett Square** fountain. Now you have an excellent view of the Trees mural (Downtown Walk I).

Walk to the **Mayo Building** located on the northwest corner of Bartlett Square. It is the earliest remaining building built by the Mayo brothers. After their rapid success in their original furniture store, they constructed this building in stages between 1910 and 1917 to provide more room for their business (For a description of the fountain and other buildings, see Downtown Walk I).

Enjoy the ambience and the waterfalls on Bartlett Square; then continue walking south on the Mall to the intersection of Sixth and Main. The building on the southwest corner of Sixth and Main Streets was designed to feature exterior lighting. Notice the cone-shaped protrusions under the second floor. The flood lights, designed to illuminate upward to projections at the top of the building, create a dramatic stage-like effect when lighted.

SOUTH ON MAIN. Continue walking south on Main Street toward Ninth Street. Before crossing Eighth Street, look to your right (west) at the spires of Holy Family Cathedral.

Another important building is located to the southeast, where you have a beautiful view of the **Boston
Avenue Methodist Church** tower. The striking feature of
the church is its 258-foot tower. Reaching upward, it
embodies the central theme of the church, "a living creation, reaching toward Light and God."

Listed among the great cathedrals of the world in the
Encyclopedia Brittanica and in the National Register of
Historic Places, Boston Avenue Methodist Church is cer-
tainly worth a special trip.

A s beautiful and inspiring as the Boston Avenue
Methodist Church is, the history of its conception and the controversy surrounding the
designers of the church are equally fascinating. The initial
architectural plans were discarded for being too traditional
and uninspiring. Adah Robinson, a Quaker and local supervi-
sor of Central High School art classes, was then contacted by the
wife of the building committee's chairman, Mrs. C. C. Cole.
Robinson steeped herself in Methodism and submitted her plans;
Pastor John A. Rice reacted initially with, "Right now I lock
horns with you." Soon afterward, however, Dr. Rice became her
greatest enthusiast and helped win over the rest of the committee.
The architectural firm of Rush, Endacott and Rush, which had

Transok light fixture

designed the Tulsa Municipal Building and the Atlas Building earlier
(Downtown Walk I), was engaged to carry out Robinson's plans. A problem subsequently arose in determining who should receive credit for the creation of the
church. Bruce Goff, the firm's young apprentice and former student of
Robinson, had been asked to interpret her design. Later, Goff became recognized
nationally while Robinson faded into obscurity. Church records—including Mrs.
Cole's "Story of the New Church," Robinson's drawings and her written philosophy for the church—clearly indicate Robinson, not Goff, as the original inspiration for the building. When the $1.5 million edifice was completed in 1929, it
was hailed as the country's first church in a strictly American style of architecture.

A TRADER'S EMPORIUM

Frank Lyon, the son of an Indian trader, bought his store (established in 1916 by Morris Simons) in 1951. It has been a popular attraction for visitors, including entertainers Sonny & Cher and opera star Roberta Peters. The Lyon family has designed beautiful feather head-dresses over the past 50 years and presented them to many important persons, starting with President Harding in 1927. Members from about half of the sixty-seven tribes that reside in Oklahoma bring their various handicrafts to the store, which specializes in war bonnets, bead-work, turquoise jewelry, Cheyenne moccasins, Navajo rugs, pottery, baskets, relics, curios of Indian Territory, and paintings by Oklahoma Indian artists.

FIRST CHRISTIAN CHAPEL. For another fine example of liturgical art, cross Ninth Street and walk through the parking lot to the chapel of **First Christian Church.** After entering the church, ask the receptionist for directions to the Memorial Chapel Sanctuary, donated by O. A. and Thelma Shaw (T.U. walk).

Upon entering the sanctuary, notice the brilliant chancel window at the far (south) end of the room. (Noon is the time to plan your visit for the best light.) Designed and fabricated by Emil Frei (Swan Lake Walk) and his group of distinguished artists and craftsmen, the window is rich in design symbolizing basic tenants of the Christian faith. The central diamond sections symbolize the Father, the Son, and the Holy Sacraments. Begin reading the chancel window from top to bottom: the Greek word Logos, meaning "the Word;" the sign of the fish symbolizing Jesus Christ; water symbolizing Baptism; grapes and loaves symbolizing the Lord's Supper. The stained glass windows on the east and west walls represent parables of Jesus and Biblical scenes. Starting with the window nearest the chapel entrance on the east wall (left) are The Prodigal Son, The Mustard Seed, Laborers in the Vineyard, and The Lost Sheep. Starting at the entrance on the west wall (right) are The Burning Bush, Jacob's Ladder, The Parable of the Soils, and The Good Samaritan.

TENTH STREET. Retrace your steps to the church's entrance and continue to the corner of Tenth Street. Look to the east where you can see the art deco tower of the old **Warehouse Market.** Recently saved by a plan worked out between the city and Home Depot, the renovated structure houses **Lyon's Indian Store,** a cornucopia of authentic Indian items.

CATHEDRAL SQUARE. Cross Tenth Street to **Cathedral Square.** Looking back toward the chapel of the First Christian Church, you have a good view of the exterior of the chancel leaded glass window. It is set in an antique bronze frame which extends into a Celtic bronze cross. The circle is emblematic of eternity and signifies the everlasting effect of the redemption secured on the cross by the death of Christ.

In the park, the **antique water fountain,** with its spreading skirt of water, contrasts with the English Gothic structure behind. The fountain's arching pattern of water lends grace to the stiff facade. Together they create a kind of European cityscape.

Enjoy resting in the park while you view the exterior of **First Methodist Church.** The upward reaches of the two limestone towers end in graceful points suggesting tapering fingers pointing heavenward. The aspiring lines lead the eye upward. Medallions of the bursting pomegranate (symbolizing the resurrection and hope of immortality) and the rose (carrying the promise of the second coming) are located on the two levels of the towers. Except for the Indiana limestone window trim and tracery, all of the stone was quarried in Oklahoma about fifteen miles from Tulsa. It is self-cleansing and does not absorb stains. The walls are solid stone, eighteen to twenty-four inches thick.

Walk to the front of the church, built between 1925-28, to view the massive **Great West Doors.** The series of graduated arches, worked in exquisite patterns of columns lead the eye forward, centering the vision on the door itself so that mind and heart receive the invitation "to enter and worship and rest in the security of the most holy faith." Just above the doors and below the stone arches in the oak panel is a series of small medallions of the vine, the rose, and the acorn, signifying latent strength and greatness. Pillars of stone on each side of the door represent the Four Gospels.

To enter the church proceed through the third entrance to the right (south). Begin your tour of the church in the **narthex,** the western entrance, and look down the **nave,** the central portion of the sanctuary. The series of Gothic arches suggests the attitude of prayer. The stately columns that support the arches are symbolic of prophets, apostles, and evangelists, who through the Christian centuries, have proven themselves to be the "Pillars of the Church." The massive and beautiful oak trusses and purlins, supporting the roof, and giving the impression of protection, are called "The Rooftree of God." The great depth of the nave suggests infinity and eternity; its great height suggests that there is a spiritual lift in joyous worship.

Proceed forward to the chancel, inner sanctuary. On the wall behind the sedilias is the reredos, or panel, a beautiful work of art in gold leaf and delicate painting in red and green. The

FIRST METHODIST: Faith in Stone

Cherubim holding the shield of faith, a symbol of the protectiveness of the church, are seen at the point where the spires join the roof of the First Methodist Church. Sturdy buttresses culminate at points in a modified form of the fleur-de-lis, representing the Holy Family. Around the eaves of the building is a series of small medallions adorned with intricate carvings of the rose, the vine (a symbol of the fruitfulness of God and the believer), and the fig leaf (symbolizing a holy life rich with the fruits of the spirit).

Pendent light fixture designed to suggest a Medieval candelabra

SYMBOLISM IN THE CHANCEL

Centered in the chancel of the First Methodist Church are the most sacred furnishings of the church beginning with the altar or communion table and its symbolic cross. The communion table is of oak (as is all the furniture and wood trim), symbolic of strength, eternity, virtue, and forgiveness. Behind the table are the five sedilias (chairs for the clergy), constructed to present unity.

designs are elaborations of the "IHS" symbol (a monogram for Jesus) and the cross and the crown, symmetrically arranged in the seven sections of the panel. In the center of the canvas and stone panel is a cross of exquisite workmanship adorned with the vine and grape, signifying "He is the vine and we are the branches."

The **Great East Window** (chancel window) is the pictorial interpretation of the last book of the New Testament, The Revelation of St. John the Divine, and suggests the redemptive work of Christ. It depicts the return of the Savior to earth, the spiritual judgment of bygone generations, the downfall and destruction of the earthly Jerusalem, and the setting up of Christ's heavenly kingdom—the new Jerusalem. The beholder's attention is centered upon the figure of the Christ represented as the King, surrounded by an aureole of glorious light and color. Plainly seen in the pictured window are the seven candlesticks borne by the seven angels, symbolic of the seven churches and the seven gifts of the Spirit found in Revelation.

While still in the chancel area, turn to face the **Great West Window**. Made of grisaille glass, it features a grey monochrome background studded with rich colors to make up a bold design. Although there is no religious symbolic significance to the patterns, the whole effect of the window is to flood the sanctuary with a rich light, contributing greatly to the sacred atmosphere. The only symbolism found in the window is in the narrow band which trims all the windows. Small sections of grey and yellow, alternated with red or blue glass, depict several designs: the flower almond, symbolic of the miraculous birth of Jesus; the mulberry, symbolic of God in nature all about us; the acorn; and the pomegranate. The best time to see the window in all its glory is at sunset, which sets it ablaze.

Leave the church and continue across the street to your car, and look once again toward downtown at the magnificent rooftops of Tulsa's buildings.

behind. The fountain's arching pattern of water lends grace to the stiff facade. Together they create a kind of European cityscape.

Enjoy resting in the park while you view the exterior of **First Methodist Church**. The upward reaches of the two limestone towers end in graceful points suggesting tapering fingers pointing heavenward. The aspiring lines lead the eye upward. Medallions of the bursting pomegranate (symbolizing the resurrection and hope of immortality) and the rose (carrying the promise of the second coming) are located on the two levels of the towers. Except for the Indiana limestone window trim and tracery, all of the stone was quarried in Oklahoma about fifteen miles from Tulsa. It is self-cleansing and does not absorb stains. The walls are solid stone, eighteen to twenty-four inches thick.

Walk to the front of the church, built between 1925-28, to view the massive **Great West Doors**. The series of graduated arches, worked in exquisite patterns of columns lead the eye forward, centering the vision on the door itself so that mind and heart receive the invitation "to enter and worship and rest in the security of the most holy faith." Just above the doors and below the stone arches in the oak panel is a series of small medallions of the vine, the rose, and the acorn, signifying latent strength and greatness. Pillars of stone on each side of the door represent the Four Gospels.

To enter the church proceed through the third entrance to the right (south). Begin your tour of the church in the **narthex**, the western entrance, and look down the **nave**, the central portion of the sanctuary. The series of Gothic arches suggests the attitude of prayer. The stately columns that support the arches are symbolic of prophets, apostles, and evangelists, who through the Christian centuries, have proven themselves to be the "Pillars of the Church." The massive and beautiful oak trusses and purlins, supporting the roof, and giving the impression of protection, are called "The Rooftree of God." The great depth of the nave suggests infinity and eternity; its great height suggests that there is a spiritual lift in joyous worship.

Proceed forward to the chancel, inner sanctuary. On the wall behind the sedilias is the reredos, or panel, a beautiful work of art in gold leaf and delicate painting in red and green. The

FIRST METHODIST: Faith in Stone

Cherubim holding the shield of faith, a symbol of the protectiveness of the church, are seen at the point where the spires join the roof of the First Methodist Church. Sturdy buttresses culminate at points in a modified form of the fleur-de-lis, representing the Holy Family. Around the eaves of the building is a series of small medallions adorned with intricate carvings of the rose, the vine (a symbol of the fruitfulness of God and the believer), and the fig leaf (symbolizing a holy life rich with the fruits of the spirit).

Pendent light fixture designed to suggest a Medieval candelabra

SYMBOLISM IN THE CHANCEL

Centered in the chancel of the First Methodist Church are the most sacred furnishings of the church beginning with the altar or communion table and its symbolic cross. The communion table is of oak (as is all the furniture and wood trim), symbolic of strength, eternity, virtue, and forgiveness. Behind the table are the five sedilias (chairs for the clergy), constructed to present unity.

designs are elaborations of the "IHS" symbol (a monogram for Jesus) and the cross and the crown, symmetrically arranged in the seven sections of the panel. In the center of the canvas and stone panel is a cross of exquisite workmanship adorned with the vine and grape, signifying "He is the vine and we are the branches."

The **Great East Window** (chancel window) is the pictorial interpretation of the last book of the New Testament, The Revelation of St. John the Divine, and suggests the redemptive work of Christ. It depicts the return of the Savior to earth, the spiritual judgment of bygone generations, the downfall and destruction of the earthly Jerusalem, and the setting up of Christ's heavenly kingdom—the new Jerusalem. The beholder's attention is centered upon the figure of the Christ represented as the King, surrounded by an aureole of glorious light and color. Plainly seen in the pictured window are the seven candlesticks borne by the seven angels, symbolic of the seven churches and the seven gifts of the Spirit found in Revelation.

While still in the chancel area, turn to face the **Great West Window.** Made of grisaille glass, it features a grey monochrome background studded with rich colors to make up a bold design. Although there is no religious symbolic significance to the patterns, the whole effect of the window is to flood the sanctuary with a rich light, contributing greatly to the sacred atmosphere. The only symbolism found in the window is in the narrow band which trims all the windows. Small sections of grey and yellow, alternated with red or blue glass, depict several designs: the flower almond, symbolic of the miraculous birth of Jesus; the mulberry, symbolic of God in nature all about us; the acorn; and the pomegranate. The best time to see the window in all its glory is at sunset, which sets it ablaze.

Leave the church and continue across the street to your car, and look once again toward downtown at the magnificent rooftops of Tulsa's buildings.

Greenwood

THE GREENWOOD WALK is through one of the most historically significant areas of Tulsa. This community, platted by city ordinance in 1909 as Northside Addition and settled by African-Americans, was destined for both turbulence and affluence.

The arrival of African-Americans in the Tulsa region had coincided with the Indian Removals of the 1830s. The five Native American tribes, which were relocated to Indian Territory from the southeastern United States during this period, included African-Americans among their numbers. Freedmen, former slaves who gained tribal membership through marriage, and slaves owned by tribal members participated in the exodus from traditional Native American homelands to the new territory.

Following the Civil War, African-Americans migrated to the Indian Territories in search of what they perceived as a functional multi-racial society. With the opening of Oklahoma and Indian Territories to commercial exploitation by means of land runs and railroads, additional numbers of African-Americans arrived in the region throughout the nineteenth century. The oil booms of the early twentieth century provided a boost to African-American migration to Oklahoma as did the decline of farming.

However, increased population and diversity brought tension and violence to Tulsa—and to this neighborhood. In 1921 a race riot completely destroyed thirty-five city blocks of the then very prosperous area known as "Black Wall Street." The death total has never been verified due to the efforts to suppress

DISTANCE

2 miles

TIME

2 hours

GREENWOOD

N

1. Mt. Zion
2. Spaghetti Warehouse
3. Cain's Ballroom
4. Brady Theater
5. Tribune
6. Bank of Oklahoma
7. Greenwood Center
8. Heritage Center
9. "When Friends Meet"
10. The Depot

details of the tragedy. This event, which was preceded by an increased level of violence directed toward African-Americans in the years following World War I, was an example of the racial violence endemic throughout the United States during the period, with the Tulsa Race Riot being possibly the most destructive example of this national trend.

Today, however, although always with the overshadowing memory of the l921 race riot, the revitalized area with its works of art, a university, and its dramatic history is a cultural gem.

MT. ZION BAPTIST CHURCH. Park in the visitors' section of the University Center at Tulsa. To begin your walk cross through **Mt. Zion Baptist Church**'s parking lot (to the left of the church). Founded in 1909, the church was originally a one-room frame structure with fifteen charter members. Later, in 1916, at a cost of $92,000 the church was rebuilt as the most stately church building in north Tulsa. No one dreamed it would stand only three months. However, during the June 1, 1921 race riot, when the apocryphal rumors spread that the Baptist church on North Elgin was being used as a place for storage of weapons and ammunition for Blacks, the church building was torched and burned. After the crazed event ended, nothing was left of Mt. Zion but the charred walls and a $50,000 mortgage. Insurance did not cover losses by war or insurrection, and the church of 200 members was advised to change its name, default the mortgage, and start over. But the congregation resolved to pay the debt, which they did.

Later, in 1952, Mt. Zion dedicated the present building, which cost more than $300,000. The church's name, when it began, was Second Baptist Church, but according to Dr. George C. McCutchen, "Folks said there was not much to be said for being 'second' in anything, and they thought about it. Someone suggested since Mt. Zion was the highest point in Jerusalem, why not rename the church 'Mt. Zion Baptist Church.' " And that is what they did.

Turn left out of the parking lot of the church and walk under the underpass until you see a field on your right. Continue walking to the end of the field where you see a parking lot. Walk through the parking lot toward the newly restored red brick with green trim building, presently the Spaghetti Warehouse.

GREENWOOD SPECIAL

JUNETEENTH ON GREENWOOD HERITAGE FESTIVAL: Third weekend in June

TULSA JAZZ FESTIVAL: Second weekend in August.

OKLAHOMA JAZZ HALL OF FAME: The Hall of Fame, at 322 North Greenwood, features historical and changing art exhibits. Call (918) 599-9966 for information.

UCT EVENTS: The University Center of Tulsa (UCT) hosts many cultural events open to the public. Call (918) 594-8000 for information.

TATE BRADY: Pioneer Builder

Brady Street was named after Tate Brady, a pioneer Tulsa builder. He constructed the old Brady Hotel on the southwest corner of Main and Archer Streets and owned one of the first mercantile stores in Tulsa. A strong booster for Tulsa's growth and active in politics, Brady was the first national committeeman of the Democratic Party from Oklahoma. In 1925, despondent over a son's death, the grief stricken Brady ended his own life.

BRICK BELT. This section of Tulsa is close to the forks of several railroads. The Midland Valley, Frisco and Missouri, Kansas and Texas were all lines that kept the warehouses in the area full and profitable. In April of 1905 the railway system had grown to the point that one enthusiastic reporter wrote, "It is possible to leave the city in nine different directions. Few cities in the country have as many railroad facilities, and none in the territory."

Now as the trains have greatly diminished in number, another industry—entertainment—has provided some of the old buildings with new life. The **Spaghetti Warehouse** restaurant has sparked a revival in the area, as it has in other cities including Oklahoma City and Dallas. Enter the lobby of the restaurant and ask to see an area in its original state so you can visit the transformation from warehouse to restaurant.

Next, turn right through the parking lot to the corner of Cincinnati Avenue and Brady Street. Just two blocks north, 401 North Cincinnati Avenue, lived the Barker clan, the most famous criminals reared in Tulsa. Ma Barker taught her four sons to "shoot, rob and never be taken alive." FBI Director J. Edgar Hoover described Ma as "the most resourceful criminal brain that America produced in that generation." The mob was responsible for kidnappings, bank robberies, and even a train holdup.

Cross to the other (south) side of **Brady Street** and continue west to Boston Avenue. Look across the street at the two- and three-story brick buildings, some of the oldest in Tulsa. (The Acme Brick Company was two blocks north of Greenwood, resulting in the wide use of brick in this area.) Now called **Brady Village**, the arts, entertainment, and retail industries are attracted to this area under a plan released by Downtown Tulsa Unlimited. Eventually, the streets will be returned to brick or brick-patterned paving inserts.

Interestingly, brick streets first appeared in Tulsa in 1907 to meet the demand for the unusual number of cars. When cars were still a rarity in the nation (Henry Ford would not begin assembly line production for another nine years), in 1905 oil-rich Tulsa boasted 205 horseless carriages.

Electric trolley cars were the transportation for most people with gasoline powered buses not appearing until 1922. And almost an anachronism in 1925, the last livery stable went quietly out of business.

Cross Boston Avenue and continue to the corner of Brady and Main Streets marked with a Bob Wills street sign. Standing on the corner with your back toward downtown, notice in the distance to the North, **Cain's Ballroom.** This famous Tulsa landmark was originally constructed as a garage in 1924 by Tate Brady and later became a dime-a-dance hall called the Louvre Ballroom. Under the ownership of Professor Madison W. Cain, "Daddy Cain," the ballroom began to flourish as Cain's Dancing Academy. Cain's started to gain international fame after Bob Wills and the Texas Playboys moved to Tulsa in 1934. Wills started a daily radio broadcast from the ballroom. Many country music legendary performers played at Cain's in its heyday—Roy Acuff, Hank Williams, Patsy Cline, and Hank Thompson.

The **El Fox Building,** dated 1906, is on the northeast corner. Later in l917, this location saw an unfortunate national trend—violent oppression of a political group—played out in Tulsa. This building housed the local chapter of the IWW-Affiliated Oil Field Workers' Union (OFWU), which had reportedly organized some 300 oil field workers in the Tulsa area under its banner. Tulsa, a pro-war, pro-oil town, was aroused by what were then considered antiwar activities. Eventually, the union was raided, members were arrested, and later, mobs following the blacked-robed leader of the "Knights of Liberty" tarred and feathered the prisoners. A full account of this event and the Tulsa race riot can be found in *Death in a Promised Land* by Scott Ellsworth.

In Oklahoma, eager to live down its frontier past, such violence brought unbelievable brutality and much embarrassment to the state. Just how many such "near lynchings" of an ethnic or

"Would I like to go to Tulsa? You bet your boots I would, Let me off at Archer, I'll walk down to Greenwood, Take me back to Tulsa."

FROM A SONG BY
BOB WILLS

THE OLD LADY ON BRADY

Built in 1914 as Tulsa's first convention hall, Brady Theatre was renamed the Municipal Theatre, and finally became known as "the Old Lady on Brady." Whatever Tulsans call her, though, she is most renowned for the stars who have graced her stage—Toscanini, Caruso, George M. Cohan, Katherine Hepburn, Helen Hayes, Pete Fountain, Beverly Sills, Mme. Pavlova, Ed Sullivan, Elvis Presley, Will Rogers . . . the list goes on. The 20,000 residents who made up Tulsa in 1913 voted a $100,000 bond issue for her construction. To put that amount in perspective, the construction superintendent was paid $5 a day, and when the convention hall was finished, the manager was hired at $100 a month.

political nature is impossible to determine. However, the state has a total of forty-one recorded lynchings in its history. Interestingly, at the very time this crime was decreasing in the United States as a whole, it was increasing in Oklahoma. Significantly, the state's early governors took strong leadership in trying to stop lynchings, and 1931 brought a welcome end to mob murder.

BRADY THEATRE. Before you leave the corner, look to your left, down the street, at Brady Theatre. Inside the theatre, the slanting stage, considered a great innovation at the time, proved a hazard for performers. One roller skater narrowly avoided the orchestra pit, and Anna Pavlova, the famous ballerina, was unprepared for the stage's slant, pirouetting so close to the orchestra pit she had to take her bows to regain her balance— long before the end of her performance.

Turn around and walk toward downtown along Main Street to **Archer Street.** This street was named for Thomas Jefferson Archer—a merchant beginning with small capital and plenty of spirit. According to legend, he "came in with the railroad gang, and his stock in trade when he opened up in Tulsa was a half barrel of cider and a box of ginger snaps." Starting out in a tent, he later built on Main Street a couple of blocks farther south and had a fine stock of hardware, furniture, groceries, and other articles. In 1894, when a drunk customer shot a random bullet into a powder keg, Archer died from the explosion.

TRIBUNE BUILDING. Beginning your return, cross Main Street and walk along the south side of Archer Street. The brick high-rise across the street is the **Tribune Building**, home to *The Tulsa Tribune* newspaper for many years. Erected in 1924, it was listed on the Register of Historic Buildings in 1979.

The *Tribune* had originally been the *Tulsa Democrat,* which itself was previously the *New Era,* founded in 1895. The weekly *New Era* had been founded by a group of Tulsa merchants who found an even earlier paper, the *Indian Chief,* too sensational. Its editor, Mr. Winegar, they believed, was not advertising the village of Tulsa properly and too many negative activities were being reported. With the *New Era,* the merchants intended to print only the positive.

Originally, the paper was printed in a small two-story building on the same land that is the site of the present building. The Tribune Building, expanded in 1929, was considered Oklahoma's largest and most modern newspaper facility. It introduced the "gravity system," a method of newspaper production in use in the rest of the nation, but previously untried in Oklahoma. Under this system, the preparation of the daily paper began on the sixth floor and progressed down through press rooms and business offices on the intermediate floors until it reached the printing presses on the first floor. The last edition of *The Tulsa Tribune* was September 30, 1992.

Architecturally, the building's symmetrical exterior is organized into four horizontal bands. The lower band, with its eight arcaded windows, forms the base. The central portion is topped by a lintel, an entablature, and a parapet wall. The classical order of the building is further delineated by brick pilasters and paired windows that emphasize the building's verticality.

Cross in the middle of the street to the doorway, framed by excellent examples of Greek Ionic columns. Above the word "Tribune" are the Greek moldings: egg and dart, and dentil.

Notice also the prominent keystone (the central stone of an arch) of each window. Although of no more structural importance than any of the other voussoirs (wedge—shaped stones) of which the arch is built, its position at the center makes it a unit that has been advantageously accented since Etruscan and Roman times.

Unfortunately, the timing of Tuesday's, May 31st, 1921 issue of the *Tribune* probably played a part in the 1921 race riot. After the initial incident between a white female elevator operator and a black male youth, the paper printed an article about "a mob of whites forming in order to lynch the Negro." The paper hit the streets at 3:15 p.m. and sometime between 6:00 and 7:00 p.m. a crowd of whites began to form outside of the courthouse, where the black youth was being held. Exact information is now impossible to obtain: *The Tulsa Tribune* microfilm file at the Tulsa City-County Library states, "Several

RICHARD LLOYD JONES

Richard Lloyd Jones, Sr., came to Tulsa in 1919 (Downtown Walk I), and purchased the then *Tulsa Democrat,* changing the name of Tulsa's first daily to *The Tulsa Tribune.* A crusading editor in an oil boom town, he continually advanced Tulsa in editorials and promotions throughout his lifetime. Jones had had several years' experience in newspaper publishing. After receiving a masters in law from Chicago Law School, he worked as editor of a Stamford, Connecticut newspaper; as an editorial writer for the *Washington Times;* as associate editor of *Cosmopolitan* magazine; and as a writer and editorialist for *Colliers* magazine. The editor's home in Tulsa, "Westhope," was designed by Jones's cousin, architect Frank Lloyd Wright. (See Sites of Interest.)

Tribune Building

Articles concerning the Race riots in the May 31: 1921 *Tribune* are missing from this paper,[sic] there are no known available copies."

BOK TOWER AREA. Walk just past the Tribune Building and look toward the Bank of Oklahoma Tower. Notice the bronze sculpture in the shape of a cloud. Actually called *Artificial Cloud,* the sculpture by Native American artist Bob Haozous has been on loan in Tulsa since the 1992 Mayfest. It weighs 1900 pounds, is seventy-two feet tall, and is made from cortin steel, intentionally meant to rust.

Continue walking to see a good view of the **Tulsa Union Depot** on your right. (See Downtown Walk I.)

Walk along Archer Street and cross Cincinnati, Detroit, and Elgin Avenues. At Frankfort Avenue look south toward the railroad tracks. Probably some of the most active fighting of the night of the 1921 race riot was along these tracks, which had always formed an important boundary between black and white Tulsa. Continue walking along Archer Street to Greenwood Avenue where other newspaper history is also located on this walk. *The Daily Tulsa Star,* edited and published by Andrew J. Smitherman, an attorney, was established in 1913 and continued to operate until 1921. Smitherman sold to Theodore Baughman, who started *The Oklahoma Eagle.* Baughman ran the newspaper until 1937 when Edward Lawrence Goodwin, Sr. purchased it. The plant was located at 122 North Greenwood, across the street from the original *Oklahoma Eagle* newspaper *The Daily Tulsa Star.*

GREENWOOD STREET. Now cross Archer Street and walk north on Greenwood Avenue. By 1908, this commercial area known as "Greenwood" was established. Merchants in the area

"RACE CLASH," 1921

The June 2, 1921 edition of the *New York Times* ran an article from Oklahoma City that read: "Evidence of the fury of the race clash was borne by a St. Louis and San Francisco passenger train which arrived here today from the East. Many of the windows in one of the coaches had been shot out and the sides of the coaches were scarred by bullets fired upon the train as it passed through the negro quarter in Tulsa early today. None of the passengers was injured."

were from such places as Arkansas, Minnesota, and Texas. Growth of this community was rapid before and after the first World War. The first two blocks comprised the heart of Tulsa's black business community, and during its heyday was referred to as the "Negro Wall Street of America." Two- and three-story brick buildings lined the avenue, housing a variety of commercial establishments, including a dry goods store, two theaters, groceries, confectioneries, restaurants, and billiard halls. A number of black Tulsa's eleven rooming houses and four hotels were located here. "Deep Greenwood" was also a favorite place for the offices of Tulsa's unusually large number of black lawyers, doctors, and other professionals.

One night of racial violence devastated the area. The riot started after a black man, Dick Rowland was accused of attacking a white female elevator operator, Sarah Page. Rumors flew through the black belt that the youth was to be lynched. Every hardware and sporting goods store in the city was broken into as the fast assembling whites armed themselves. Confrontations between black and white Tulsans at the County Court House occurred twice during the evening of May 31st. The second confrontation became violent when shots were fired and the outnumbered blacks began retreating to the business area centered at Archer and Greenwood. In the early

JAZZ

Viewing the art as you pass through the underpass, reflect on the historic significance of America's most famous indigenous music—jazz. Jazz, a fusion of African rhythms filtered through European instruments, was transported to the United States via black slaves. Jazz has its genesis in work songs, field hollers, railroad crew chants, church shouts, spirituals, and blues; all part of the folk heritage of a people subjected to slavery.

morning hours of June 1st, thirty-five blocks of Tulsa's African-American community were systematically looted and burned by the white mob. Businesses, schools, residences, and churches were all put to the torch.

Property losses in the neighborhood were estimated to be $2.3 million. The total number of people who died in the riot is in question; estimates range from 27 to over 250. The figure of 75 persons is accepted by some authorities as most accurate.

Rowland was never formally charged with assault, and Page left Tulsa shortly after the riot without pressing charges.

The entire commercial area, now known as Greenwood Street, was rebuilt after the riot. Old businesses were reestablished and new businesses were started. New churches and schools were constructed on their former sites. Later, as desegregation and integration came into effect, the area again suffered economic loss as black capital was dispersed throughout the city instead of being concentrated in the Greenwood area. The seventies found only two businesses left in Deep Greenwood—The *Oklahoma Eagle* and the law offices of E. L. Goodwin, Sr. Today, however, the area is again revitalized to prove the value of its culture and endurance of its history.

This area is listed in the Oklahoma Landmarks Inventory and is worthy of designation as a site in the National Register for its historic associations. The buildings themselves have been

rehabilitated in the past ten years keeping the National Register criteria in mind.

Because it was a geographic crossroads, Oklahoma served as a melting pot for both the New Orleans "Dixieland" and East coast music, and during the "Jazz Age," Greenwood's various clubs and speakeasies were gathering places for musicians.

Leaving the underpass you will notice the **Greenwood Cultural Center** and the **Mabel B. Little Heritage House** on your left. Originally, the home was built by the Mackey family who were owners of more than 1000 homes destroyed in the riot. In 1926 they rebuilt; however, this time they vowed that their home would never again be destroyed by fire and rebuilt in brick. Later, in the 1980s, at a cost of $100,000 the house was brought to this location. Today, due to the inspiration of Mabel B. Little, Opal Dargan, and Thelma Whitlow, the house is a museum depicting North Tulsa's history through art, photographs, and posters.

UCT. Follow the sidewalk in front of the pond to explore the **University Center at Tulsa,** which contracts with four state universities —The University of Oklahoma, Oklahoma State University, Northeastern State University, and Langston University. Proceed first to the new addition, at the far end.

On the exterior of the new addition are breathtaking tile murals created by local artist Ruth Armstrong. Randle first envisioned something "light and airy" around several of the entrances, but when Armstrong produced her drawings tying into Tulsa's art deco history, Randle and the board wanted to put her work everywhere, and so they did. Armstrong's inspiration came from the buildings downtown, the fairgrounds, the old Woolworth building, and other torn down art deco structures. The colors are brighter but still part of the art deco palette. She received help painting over 3,000 tiles from ten of her women friends, a process that was labor intensive as each tile

UCT

UCT's first classes were held in Tulsa's state office building. Then Tulsans voted $15,000,000 in building funds and committed land to provide a campus. When the 1988 building opened on this site, it represented the largest single contribution of a city to state higher education in the history of Oklahoma. In 1995 UCT opened its spectacular new addition. President Rodger Randle said that the board "wanted a people-scaled place that integrated the indoors with the outdoors — architecture that promoted the creation of community" and the village, designed by architectural firm HTB, has successfully fulfilled the board's vision. Randle insists that there will be no institutional cafeteria as in most universities; instead, small eating places with outdoor areas invite friendly conversation.

has five coats of paint, and the two kilns used for the firing could hold only eighteen tiles each.

The hard work of Randle, Armstrong, and the UCT board was well worth the effort for the European-like space with its beautiful stairway, fountains, and plantings is one of the most inviting people places in Tulsa. Plan to linger awhile in the area, have a snack, and visit the theatre inside where interior decorator J. Richard Neel used seats from a 1920s theatre and continued the art deco colors.

To return to your car, walk under the colonnade toward the original building. Be sure to notice the seemingly abstract tiles on each of the buildings that ties the new addition to the old and is the letter "T" for Tulsa.

Inside the original building, terraces offer excellent locations to enjoy panoramic views of downtown. The northeast entrance of the original structure hosts a piece of art truly worth the walk—a bronze sculpture by Allan Houser (Gilcrease Walk). Perhaps this work, more than any words that can be spoken, exemplifies the new spirit of Greenwood's future—it is entitled *When Friends Meet.*

Maple Ridge

F OR A GLIMPSE AT TULSA'S PAST, take a walk
through historic Maple Ridge. Once considered "the
wrong side of the tracks," Maple Ridge is now an energetic
residential neighborhood boasting a variety of differently styled
homes. Expect to see examples of neoclassic, Gothic Tudor,
Jacobethan, Italianate, Georgian, and Colonial Revival, plus
Prairie, bungalow, and cottage style homes set on spacious,
beautifully landscaped sites. A register of the first residents of
Maple Ridge reads like an early Who's Who List of Tulsa. Most
of the big names in oil and banking, including W. G. Skelly,
Harry Tyrell, and Waite Phillips, were residents of the area
called "Black Gold Row." This development, which now
includes the neighborhoods between Peoria Avenue and the
River Park's bike path, Fifteenth Street and Twenty-ninth
Street, was the first area in Indian Territory, and later,
Oklahoma, to be designed exclusively for larger, more expensive
homes.

The story of Maple Ridge begins with the famous Glenn
Pool oil strike in 1905 and the people who came to Tulsa from
the East to take advantage of the "black gold." Many of the early
successful people—the Archers, the Kennedys, the Bradys, and
the Owens—built their grand homes on the north side of town.
But by 1912, the year of the big Cushing oil strike, sites were
becoming less available in the prestigious sections of town. At
that time Maple Ridge was unappealing farm land. Seventy-five
acres located east of the railroad tracks and north of Twenty-first
Street, it contained one small orchard and one large native oak

WALK I

DISTANCE

1+ miles

TIME

1.5 hours

WALK II

DISTANCE

1+ miles

TIME

1.5 hours

tree. Besides the lack of appeal, the area was too far south to be connected with the trolly system, which stopped at Eleventh Street. The developers who bought the land had to entice people to buy by offering lots cheaply, in addition to giving prizes of twenty-dollar gold pieces. Final acceptance of the area eventually came when such civic leaders as Congressman Bird McGuire built their fine homes on this treeless prairie.

Today, with the tree-lined streets and the landscaped medians along Madison Boulevard, the desolate prairie of the early years is hard to imagine. The original residents of Maple Ridge worked hard to make their homes beautiful, and this same spirit is alive today. During the late 1960s and early 1970s, the homeowners banded together to fight a planned expressway which threatened their neighborhood. The homeowners, who fought a seven-year battle with city, state, and federal governments, were labeled "willful obstructionists" by many; their tenacity, however, preserved an historic neighborhood with a bike path in place of the proposed expressway. In 1983 this area was placed on the National Register of Historic Places.

1728 South Madison Boulevard

W A L K   I

MADISON BOULEVARD AND 19TH STREET. The first Maple Ridge walk takes you through the original seventy-five acres owned by John T. Kramer, who named the area after the many maple trees he planted, and ends with a visit to the Fenster Gallery of Jewish Art.

Begin your walk at **1723 South Madison Boulevard.** This Italianate-styled home, built in 1917, is typical of many area homes that tried to duplicate grand architectural styles of Europe. It is an impressive home with a large front veranda surrounded by a balustrade. Imagine how incongruous this home, beautifully situated now, seemed on a treeless prairie lot.

Contrast this home with the much more simply styled home across the street at **1728 South Madison.** This second home, constructed in 1919, is an adaptation of Frank Lloyd Wright's Prairie Style house.

Prominent white bands with the unusual feature of a scrolled frieze ornamentation emphasize the horizontal lines of the home. A nice contrast to the Italianate across the street, the home is asymmetrical. Although the high ceilings inside are not apparent from the street, notice the large amount of space between the windows and the roof line. Other interesting features are the brick pilasters, which highlight the structural points of the house and also give to the design a sense of rhythm. As in beats of music, there are two columns, a space, then one more column. The original resident, a Tulsa oil operator, was innovative in his choice of an American rather than European style for the exterior of his home.

Walk south on Madison Boulevard to 18th Street and turn left (east) to **1030 East 18th Street.** Although the construction of "Huntleigh" began in the fall of 1914, the foundation was allowed to settle until spring before work continued. The Dan Hunt family moved into the completed home in May of 1916. Influenced by Greek and Georgian styles, the home is patterned

"We of the Middle West are living on the Prairie. The prairie has a beauty of its own and we should recognize and accentuate this natural beauty, its quiet level. Hence, gently sloping roofs, low proportions, quiet sky lines, suppressed heavy-set chimneys and sheltered overhangs, low terraces and out-reaching walls sequestering private gardens."

FRANK LLOYD WRIGHT

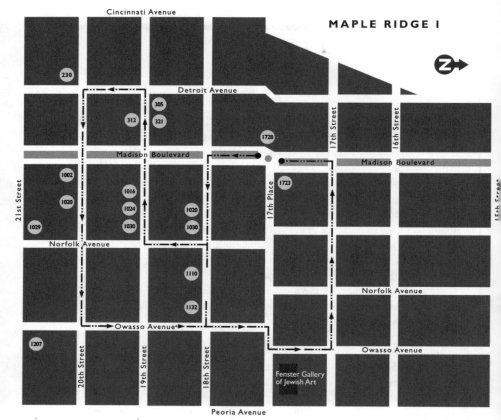

MAPLE RIDGE I

MAPLE RIDGE I

after a plantation which Mr. Hunt saw near Joplin, Missouri. John Winkler, a noted local architect (Downtown Walks I and II), drew plans based on Mr. Hunt's ideas for the home. The outstanding features are the six, 35-foot Doric columns. The cypress wood columns were "dressed" in Louisiana and shipped to Tulsa on railroad flat cars. Until the pillars were installed, huge timbers resembling telephone poles supported the portico. The size of the columns is further accentuated by the entryway, relatively small for this size home. Beneath the triangular pediment, notice the trygliphs alternating with blank metope areas, architectural features derived from the Greek Parthenon.

Another Greek motif includes the dentil-styled frieze that encircles the home. Hunt personally selected all of the lumber for the house; the bricks, which are extra dense and about six to seven pounds each, were custom-made for the house. Including verandas and basement the home is 10,000 square feet.

During the tragic race riot of 1921 (Greenwood Walk), the W. E. Browns, who owned "Huntleigh" at that time, hid twenty-five African-Americans in their basement. As "round-ups" were being staged to bring in agitators, many of the residents of Maple Ridge hid their cooks and chauffeurs as well as the servants' families and friends. Hunt built the home next door to the right at **1020 East 18th Street** for his daughter. He gave the lot to her for a wedding present. Although much smaller than "Huntleigh," the home is similar in style.

Walk across Norfolk Avenue to **1110 East 18th Street.** Notice how much wider the entryway is compared to "Huntleigh"'s. Another prominent feature includes the stone quoins edging the front wall junctions. The large windows in front are crowned by flat lintels with pronounced keystones.

THE HUNTS OF HUNTLEIGH

Dan Hunt founded Hunt's Department Store, which later became Brown-Dunkin and is now Dillard's. In 1903 his wife, Bessie, who helped found Trinity Episcopal Church, held the first service for Trinity Church in their former home located on the site of the Williams Green (Downtown Walk I). In 1905 she helped select the present site for the church. The Hunts sold their home, but later repurchased it from the W. E. Browns, only to lose it in 1939 during the Depression.

"Huntleigh,"
1030 East
18th Street

The developer of Maple Ridge almost went broke trying to sell lots because, according to builder John T. Blair, "No woman of any importance socially would live across the tracks."

Doric pilaster, 1030 East 19th Strreet

Transom lights, the small glass sections above the main doors, were often used as a source of ventilation. The horizontal and vertical lines of the home are interrupted by the lunnets over the dormer windows and the curved trim over the dormers' roofs. The steep double-pitched roof and straight-sided gable, crowned by a chimney at each end, classify this home, built in 1916, as a version of the Dutch Colonial style.

One of the early owners was James J. McGraw, President of the Exchange National Bank, which under his leadership became recognized as the "Oil Bank of America." During World War I, McGraw, as director of the National Board of the Knights of Columbus, organized and directed relief work in Belgium and France. Because of his distinguished service, he received the Order of Leopold from the Belgium King and was knighted by the French Government and by Pope Benedict. Locally, McGraw was a leader in promoting commercial air traffic in Tulsa, and under his stimulus, Tulsa's airport had more commercial air service than any other airport in the world at that time. When McGraw died, President Calvin Coolidge, Herbert Hoover, and other distinguished people sent condolences.

After viewing the McGraw home, return to Norfolk Avenue and walk south to 19th Street. Turn right (west) at the corner. The home at **1030 East 19th Street** originally belonged to Grant Stebbins, the major owner and developer of the Maple Ridge Addition. John T. Kramer sold his farm land to Stebbins in 1914. Stebbins almost went broke trying to sell the lots because according to builder John T. Blair, "No woman of any importance socially would live across the tracks." Fortunately for Stebbins, because land west of the tracks was completely developed, people coming to Tulsa during the oil boom were forced to other areas of town. Stebbins induced Congressman Bird McGuire to build in Maple Ridge by giving him a free lot. Soon afterward other prominent people followed suit. Stebbins was also instrumental in establishing a university in Tulsa. Because of Stebbins's gift of land, Henry Kendall College, forerunner of the University of Tulsa, moved here from Muskogee (University of Tulsa Walk). Stebbins later helped raise $1,000,000 so the new university could stay open. Stebbins subsequently sold his home

to Ralph Talbot, the owner of every major private
vaudeville and movie theater in Tulsa, including
the Orpheum, which hosted such greats as Al
Jolson, Mae West, and W. C. Fields.

The 1915 Stebbins/Talbot home features architectural motifs from a variety of
styles, including Doric-styled pilasters on
either side of the porch, Doric
columns on the second floor, dentil molding, and projecting dormers on either side
of the triangular-shaped pediment.

As a wedding gift, Stebbins gave the
land next door at **1024 East 19th Street** to
his daughter. Her husband, R. Otis
McClintock, was established as Chairman of
the Board of First National Bank by Waite
Phillips in 1925. Under McClintock's leadership the bank's assets grew to over $700
million.

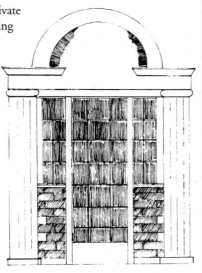

Palladian entrance,
1024 East 19th Street

The Palladian entrance of the home predominates. In contrast to "Huntleigh"'s entrance, it is much larger in relation to
the mass of the house. The home also sits farther back on the
land. Symmetry is achieved by wing extensions on both sides
and by an arched screen porch window, balancing the arched
window on the west. (During the Depression, the McClintocks
built another home on the northwest corner of 41st Street and
Lewis Avenue. A copy of a French chateau, the home, designed
by John Duncan Forsythe, is still one of the most beautiful and
impressive estates in Tulsa.)

Continuing westward, at **1016 East 19th Street**, is a well-
proportioned home built in 1921 by William L. Kistler, a
prominent oil executive. Contrasted in style with "Huntleigh,"
the one-story fluted Ionic columns of the Kistler entrance produce a dramatically different effect. The entryway is further
adorned by a Palladian window, more columns, and a prominent balustrade. Notice the small round window located in the
center front gable.

Farther west on 19th Street across Madison Boulevard, the

HARRY TYRELL: A Green Lawn and the Gift of Music

Harry Tyrell, one of the first two owners of the house at 305 East 19th Street, imported sod blocks from California and thus had the first year-round green lawn in Tulsa. A major supporter of the University of Tulsa, Tyrell helped make possible the music building that bears his name. The second of the first two owners of the house, Presley G. Walker, also supported the university. In his will, Walker permanently endowed a history chair. Tyrell and Presley both made their money in oil.

home at **321 East 19th Street**, built in 1919, was owned by Otto Kramer, nephew of John T. Kramer. Otto, part owner of Maple Ridge area, owned the original orchard on this land, which is believed to have been planted by the Perryman family, pioneer Creek Indian settlers (Brookside Walk).

Across the street at **312 East 19th Street**, a home built in 1919, is a duplicate of a Chicago home designed by Frank Lloyd Wright in 1909. Note the quintessential, leaded glass Wright windows on the east and west wings.

On the northwest corner of 19th Street and Detroit Avenue at **305 East 19th Street** is another example of Georgian Colonial. The colossal portico is very similar in style to "Huntleigh"'s entrance. Major differences include Ionic columns and an arched doorway. Beveled, leaded tracery glass flanks the door, which is topped by a fanlight window. Notice the unusual curved corners of the front door. Dentil molding is located under the scroll-like medallions, ornamental blocks under the eaves. Built in 1914, this home was one of the earliest built in the Maple Ridge area.

EAST 20TH STREET. Turn left (south) at Detroit Avenue and walk to the home on the corner at **230 East 20th Street**, highlighted by a semicircular portico. Built in 1921 by J. W. Beyer, a prominent builder, the home features influences from the Georgian and Adam style architecture. The Adam style, sometimes called the Federal style, takes its name from three brothers who had the biggest architectural practice in England from 1730 - 1780. The first example of this style found in the United States is in the ceiling, crafted in 1775, in George Washington's dining room at Mount Vernon. As explained by Robert Adam, the novelty of the brothers' interior design lay in ". . . its substitution of a beautiful variety of light moulding, gracefully formed, delicately enriched and arranged with propriety and skill." Qualities of the Adam style are also evident on the exterior of this house. The columns are spaced farther apart than ones seen before and produce a light and airy feeling. Other Adam's features include the semi-elliptical fanlight over the doorway and the sidelights flanking the door. Notice the small amount of space reserved for the narrow windows, accentuating the height of the house. Another interesting touch is the plaster cartouche between the windows above the front door.

Continue east on 20th Street to **1002 East 20th Street**, another example of the Adam style influence. This home seems broader and more massive when compared to the previous home. More space is devoted to windows, the portico stops at the second floor, and the front entrance is more elevated. The home also exhibits a hipped roof with a dormer window. Henry Ketchum built the home in about 1920. He was an enterprising man who took advantage of the famous Cushing oil field. By 1915 the field was producing 300,000 barrels of oil per day. The Oklahoma Attorney General ruled that oil was a natural resource and could not be shipped out of state until after it had been refined. As there were insufficient refining facilities in the state at that time, much of this oil flowed over the ground and into creek beds. Ketchum, after acquiring some creek bottom acreage outside the area of the producing leases, moved his mules and equipment to Cushing, where he dammed some of these creeks to impound the oil which he claimed and eventually sold to Oklahoma refineries for a reported $500,000. Later,

By 1915 the Cushing oil field was producing 300,000 barrels per day. The Oklahoma Attorney General ruled that oil could not be shipped from Oklahoma in its unrefined state but refinery capacity was insufficient so oil was released into creek beds. Ketchum dammed the creeks, impounded the oil, and sold it to state refineries for half a million dollars.

Semi-circular portico, 230 East 20th Street

The Exchange National Bank, forerunner of the Bank of Oklahoma, was organized in 1910 by thirty of Tulsa's wealthiest men. It prevented a Rockefeller and Mellon monopoly in the petroleum industry and was one of the major reasons that Tulsa became the Oil Capital of the World.

he returned to Tulsa to build this home and to operate the Hotel Tulsa, the financial hub of the Mid-Continent Oil Field operations.

East at **1020 East 20th Street** is another mixture of Late Georgian and Adam style. The home was built in 1917 by Arthur Newlin, Vice-President and Secretary of the Exchange National Bank, forerunner of the Bank of Oklahoma (Downtown Walk I). The bank, organized in 1910 by thirty of Tulsa's wealthiest men, including Harry F. Sinclair, financed independent oil producers, thereby preventing a Rockefeller and Mellon monopoly in the petroleum industry. The policies of Exchange National Bank were one of the major reasons that Tulsa became the Oil Capital of the World.

MCGUIRE HOME. From this home continue east on 20th Street to Owasso Avenue. Turn left and walk two blocks north to **1132 East 18th Street.** Built in 1915, the McGuire home was the drawing card for many other influential families into this area. Bird McGuire, the first owner and original builder, began his career as a range rider in Indian Territory. He later authored the enabling bill for statehood and became the first congressman to represent Oklahoma in Washington, D. C. After deciding not to seek reelection, McGuire chose Tulsa for his law practice. No lots were available in the prestigious Stonebreaker Heights, west of the Midland Valley Tracks in the Riverview neighborhood. McGuire contacted John T. Blair, an architect and noted builder, to request his assistance in finding a lot and designing a home. On the advice of Blair, Stebbins, the Maple Ridge developer, offered the entire block for only $6,000 upon consideration that McGuire build a house of substantial size and proportions. Mrs. McGuire wanted the home to reflect the place which had been so good for her husband's career. She said the home was "to look like Oklahoma . . . the exterior completely in native stone." She and Blair hand-picked every stone from the Osage Hills and had them hauled daily by mule-drawn wagons. Unfortunately, Mrs. McGuire disliked the completed home; it was sold in 1916 to Ben Rice at a substantial profit.

The continuing saga of the "McGuire Home" reads like a

poorly written soap opera. Soon after purchasing the home, Rice left his wife and children for Mrs. Oglesby, who was married to a wealthy oil man reportedly a member of the English royal family. Rice, guilt-ridden, committed suicide on his father's grave in Tulsa. Mr. Oglesby, grieving over his wife's desertion, died, leaving his entire estate, valued at $10,000,000, to his sixteen-year-old niece, Katherine Cornell. Katherine became the largest single stockholder of Texaco. (The St. John Alcohol Treatment Center is named in her honor.)

From 1973 until 1975, the McGuire Home was part of the vast real estate holdings of the Reverend Sun Myung Moon and his notorious religious cult. The young Moonies were required to sleep on the floor in sleeping bags and to remove their shoes before entering the house. When the Reverend Moon visited Tulsa, he stayed in the mansion in fulfillment of a requirement of the cult that Moon live in luxury while his followers take a vow of poverty. The Moonies departed Tulsa after the city enforced the single family zoning requirements.

FENSTER MUSEUM. After you have finished viewing the McGuire Home, continue north on Owasso Avenue for one block; turn right (east) on 17th Place and walk to the entrance of **The Fenster Museum of Jewish Art** at 1223 East 17th Place.

After you leave the museum, walk to 17th Street and notice the parking lot across the street. It was once the site of Waite Phillips's first Tulsa home, which he and his family occupied until they built Villa Philbrook.

To return to your car, walk west on 17th Street to Madison Boulevard.

menorah

FENSTER MUSEUM OF JEWISH ART

LOCATION: 1223 East 17th Place

HOURS: Sunday-Thursday, 10-4

Founded in 1966 by a private endowment to memorialize Gershon and Rebecca Fenster, the museum contains outstanding collections of Judaica, including an eighteenth-century, silk Torah curtain, a brass cabinet for storing ritual objects, and a silver and brass Polish Torah crown from the eighteenth century. Some of these extraordinary objects are nearly four thousand years old. The museum is also a repository for the Oklahoma Jewish Archives and location of the National Council of Jewish Women's Holocaust Education Center. For information about the museum or Docent-led tours, call **(918) 582-3732.**

WILLIAM G. SKELLY: Sassy Chief

The Osage Indians dubbed the colorfully outspoken Skelly Wah-Tah-in-Kah, "Sassy Chief" or "one who speaks up for his Indian friends." His other friends called him "Mr. Tulsa." He contributed greatly to Tulsa's growth by helping to form the Tulsa Airport Corporation, underwritten by a "stud horse note"—a financing technique which was simply a slip of paper signed by as many citizens as the bank deemed adequate, none of whom could pay at the time but all of whom were confident that one of them, "a stud horse," would step forward to pay when the note came due. Skelly was also instrumental in forming the Spartan Aircraft Company, the Skelly Stadium, and the radio station KVOO (Voice of Oklahoma).

W A L K   I I

In the 1920s people were lured to Maple Ridge by the prospect of finding a silver tea service or a gold piece, treasures in a hunt staged by real estate developers Al Farmer and A. E. Duran. As further encouragement to buy land there, these developers advertised the addition as being the only one in Tulsa with regular mail delivery. Today, the stately houses of this impressive neighborhood indicate the success of those promotional schemes. And the tree-lined boulevards, winding streets, and meticulously landscaped lawns lure people, especially walkers.

SKELLY MANSION. Begin your walk at the corner of 21st Street and Madison Boulevard in front of the Skelly Mansion at **2101 South Madison Boulevard.** William G. Skelly's story is typical of the young, ambitious men who were attracted to Tulsa because of its oil and who stayed and left their mark by building palatial homes and participating in philanthropic deeds. Skelly began as a tool dresser in Erie, Pennsylvania. During the next twenty years, he worked his way west organizing oil companies and selling them for substantial profits. (During the period of his greatest success, he was worth more than $600 million.) He moved to Tulsa in 1912 and, in 1919, organized Skelly Oil Company, which later became one of the world's largest independent oil companies. Skelly subsequently became involved in a decade-long skirmish with J. Paul Getty, who had begun his career in Tulsa as a wildcatter. The oil companies of Skelly and Getty officially merged in January, 1977—seven months after Getty's death and twenty years after Skelly's.

In about 1921 Skelly bought this 25-

room, neoclassical home while it was still under construction. It is reported that the home was completed for $250,000. The architect, John T. Blair, recalled in a 1975 interview having one day decided that he had "just spent enough" of Skelly's money and he told him so. "Blair," said Skelly, "my wife has never asked me to take her to Europe or buy her a summer home on Long Island. If she can find something out there to put into that house that she likes, and I can afford to pay it, I don't think it's anybody else's business."

The things that Skelly could afford included a bank vault from Kansas City, two Baccarat crystal chandeliers imported from Europe, seven mantels—one of black solid marble—and gold-plated fixtures for Mrs. Skelly's bathroom. Later, in 1927 Mr. Skelly had a forty-foot dining room added to the house so

"My wife has never asked me to take her to Europe or buy her a summer home on Long Island," said Skelly. "If she can find something to put into that house that she likes, and I can afford to pay it, I don't think it's anybody else's business."

Skelly Mansion, 2101 South Madison Boulevard

Pediment adorned
with dentil molding,
at 2119 South
Madison Boulevard

"*I always stayed
with the theory
that if
Europeans
could build
houses that
would stand up
for 300 years
and still be
serviceable, we
should be able
to build houses
that people
don't have to
start repairing
ten years after
they're built.*"

JOHN BLAIR

that
he and his wife could entertain
large groups of dignitaries from around the world. The
mansion was willed to the University of Tulsa on Skelly's death
in 1957. Two years later the university sold it. From 1968 to
1978 James R. Jones, the United States Representative from
Oklahoma's First District, lived in the home. It was later
restored and included in the National Register of Historic
Places in 1978.

The exterior of the home includes a monumental two-story
portico supported by cut stone columns with lotus-styled capi-
tols. A transom of clear leaded glass adorns the severe front
door. Flanking the entrance are carriage lights, believed to have
come from an early-day hearse. On either side of the portico is
a pair of double French doors opening onto the terrace; a fanlight crowns each doorway.

John Blair also designed and supervised the construction of
the home next door at **2119 South Madison Boulevard**.
Seventy years later this home is a testament to Blair's philoso-
phy of durability. He built this home in 1923 for Roy B.
Thompson, Vice-President of Mid-Continent Building
Company and Thompson Brothers Oil Company (Downtown
Walk I).

Although more ornate than a standard Georgian house, the
home exhibits hallmarks of Georgian design in its solid geometric proportions with a centered entrance and in the contrast
between the white trim and the red brick facade. The sash windows, another Georgian element, are enhanced by their prominent keystones. The formal home is enriched with classical
details; a pediment adorned with dentil molding is centered
over a Palladian-styled entrance displaying Ionic columns.
Changes to the home include the stained glass windows flanking the arched pseudo window. Also, a wing was added to the

south, thereby easing the rigid symmetry of the original structure.

F. B. Parriot, the nationally known oilman and executive committee chairman of Sunray Mid-Continent Oil Company who bought the home in 1927, imported European sterling silver and crystal light fixtures signed by the designers. The Parriots lived in this home until they moved to their ten-acre estate in Forest Hills on the northwest corner of 31st Street and Lewis Avenue.

HISTORIC HOMES OF MAPLE RIDGE. Directly across the street to the south at **1008 Sunset Drive** is a home that originally belonged to Roberta Campbell Lawson. The charming pink and white house across Madison at **2202 South**

MAPLE RIDGE II

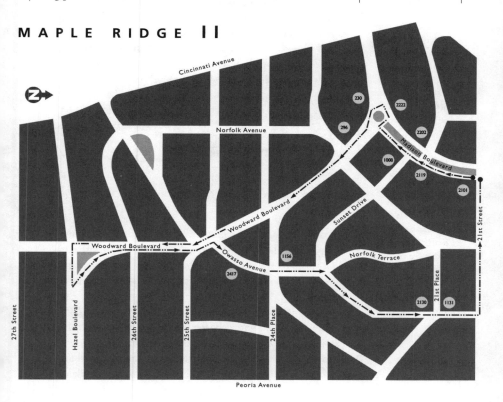

ROBERTA CAMPBELL LAWSON: Collector

Roberta Campbell Lawson was descended from the last tribal chief of the Delaware Indians, the Reverend Charles Journey Cake. Mrs. Lawson's tireless efforts in behalf of culture brought her many honors, including induction into the Oklahoma Hall of Fame. She was an enthusiastic collector of Indian objects of art. In 1947, six years after her death, Roberta's only son, Edward C. Lawson, gave her collection to Philbrook Museum of Art. The gift included over one thousand different items: Native American clothing, jewelry, beadwork, plus more than one thousand rare volumes of historical value (Philbrook Museum of Art Walk).

Madison Boulevard was designed by George Winkler (Downtown Walks I and II) and built about 1923 for oilman James P. Flanagan. Flanagan, referred to as Harry Sinclair's right-hand man, was president of Sinclair Oil Company of Louisiana before he settled in Tulsa. The house, copied after one in Italy, boasts a dining room which is a small replica of the Hall of Mirrors in the Palace of Versailles. Although appearing to be only one story as it telescopes outward to the corner, the home is actually two stories. Italianate features include the use of arches, the arcaded front porch, very wide eaves supported by large paired brackets, and a multi-colored tile roof supporting a parapet wall. Tall, thin arched windows, another hallmark of the Italianate, are simulated by French doors crowned by the use of a semi-circular window; the fan-light design is carried out over other windows by a recessed facade. The spiral columns suggest a Renaissance influence.

Walk next door to **2222 South Madison Boulevard**, built in 1921 by the area's developer, Al Farmer. The Italian Renaissance styled home, which took one year to build, was constructed with such care that there are no interior or exterior cracks. Meticulously preserved by the present owner, the home retains many of its origi-

Parapet with carved festoons, 2222 South Madison Boulevard

nal amenities, including plaster cornices, elaborate molding and paneling, hand-painted murals, and the still-in-use outdoor sprinkler system. George Winkler not only designed the home but provided elaborate instructions for its many interesting features.

The entrance is very formal with a Palladian entry door crowned by a fanlight and deep molding embellished with carvings. Over the portico is a parapet decorated with carved festoons. Most notable on the exterior are the four marble Corinthian columns of the portico with half-columns flanking the doorway and squared columns at the corners.

Dr. Fred S. Clinton, eminent early Tulsan, lived in the house across the street at **230 Woodward Boulevard**. After beginning his medical career in 1895 at Red Fork, Dr. Clinton moved his practice to Tulsa three years later. His role during the 1900 severe smallpox epidemic (Tulsa population 1,390) convinced him of the urgent need for better public health facilities. By 1905 he was building Tulsa's first permanent hospital and nurses' training school, and in 1915 he led in the construction of Tulsa's first modern hospital—now the Oklahoma Osteopathic Hospital.

From the Clinton home go to your left (south) and stroll along Woodward Boulevard to the house on your right at **296 Norfolk Avenue**. The 1927 home is best viewed from the corner. Influences unique to the Spanish Colonial Revival style include the red tiled, low pitched roof and the balconies of wrought iron. Common to this style is the varied treatment of windows; square, leaded glass windows are on the west side while arched windows flanked by limestone columns are on the east. Notice how the side walls of the house extend outward to enclose the back yard.

Continue along Woodward Boulevard across 24th Place and turn back to view the four new homes at the intersection of Woodward and 24th Place. Originally this was the site of a Georgian Colonial mansion, the first home erected south of 21st Street, built by Lionel E. Z. Aaronson in 1918. Aaronson, Secretary-Treasurer of the Midco Oil Company, one of the first oil companies formed during the discovery of the Mid-Continent field, was interested in the orderly growth of Tulsa. Recognizing Tulsa's need for beautiful areas of residential development, Aaronson acquired land south of 21st Street and built over twenty homes in the Maple Ridge area. Known as a Hebrew scholar, Aaronson included a synagogue in his home for his family and neighbors because the only other synagogue in Tulsa was not within walking distance.

In 1972 the home was bought by rock musician Leon Russell who lived in the home for several years. The destruction of the mansion in the 1980s was an impetus for the creation of

FRED CLINTON: Physician and Publicist

In the annals of Tulsa history, Fred Clinton is remembered for setting into motion the event that would change Tulsa forever. A partner with Dr. J. C. Bland in the 1901 Sue Bland oil well, Dr. Clinton initiated the publicity about the discovery which spread nationwide. The news sprang into headlines throughout the country— "Greatest Oil Well West of the Mississippi." "A Geyser of Oil Spouts at Red Fork." The well's modest production of 100 barrels a day was boosted by the press to 30,000; it became, in imagination, a "great gusher," spouting over 400 feet into the air. Independent producers and big oil companies swarmed to the new field and started the chain of events that would ultimately make Tulsa the Oil Capital of the World.

Hazel Boulevard was named for developer Al Farmer's daughter. Exhibiting motifs from a variety of styles — English Tudor, French Provincial, and Georgian Colonial — its stately homes from the late twenties, sitting far back on their expansive lawns, make this block one of the most elegant and appealing streets in Tulsa.

Historic Preservation Zoning. An ordinance led to the creation of the Tulsa Preservation Commission, which now reviews demolition and new construction in designated areas to determine the appropriateness of the proposal.

Continue walking south on Woodward Boulevard, past several small median islands, to the largest island at Hazel Boulevard. This wide street was named after developer Al Farmer's daughter. If you have time, you might enjoy walking east on Hazel Boulevard. Exhibiting motifs from a variety of styles—English Tudor, French Provincial, and Georgian Colonial—these stately homes from the late twenties, sitting far back on their expansive lawns, make this block one of the most elegant and appealing streets in Tulsa.

At the island, retrace your steps along Woodward Boulevard to Owasso Avenue. Turn right and walk to the grey shingled home, built in 1948, at **2417 South Owasso Avenue**. Reminiscent of an eighteenth-century New England home, the proportion and detail of this home contribute to its charm. The white picket fence and the juxtaposition of crisp white trim against grey wooden shingles are in keeping with the Cape Cod style. The white frame around the front door is copied from a 1680 home, reported to be one of the oldest houses on Long Island.

Continue from here to 24th Place. Walk to the front of **1156 East 24th Place**, a home built in 1920 by a leading Oklahoma banker and financier, W. E. Brown. Although the symmetry evident in this home is not characteristic of the English Tudor styling, such features as half timbering and cutouts on the stucco facade, leaded glass windows, and a sloping roof line are typical of English Tudor homes. The front doorway is recessed; the brick portico is trimmed in carved limestone. Inside, the entrance hall rises two stories and the herringbone-patterned oak floors are bordered by walnut.

From here, continue along Owasso Avenue for a short block. Then at the junction of three streets, follow the street to the extreme right which is a continuation of Owasso Avenue. At the end of the block on your left is **2130 Owasso Avenue** built in 1919. Notice how the home addresses the corner loca-

tion by having two prominent entrances. Although the main doorway faces 21st Place, the side entrance is more elaborate with its portico supported by massive Corinthian columns.

Irish cottage at 1207 East 21st Street

The home across 21st Place at **1131 East 21st Place** exhibits architectural motifs from a variety of styles. The proportion of the home is Georgian, but the green tiled roof and balustrade surrounding the front porch suggest Italianate influences. Both Italianate and French Provincial influences are combined in the front entry.

Follow Owasso Avenue to 21st Street and look across the street to the "Irish Cottage" on the corner at **1207 East 21st Street.** (Winter is the best time to view this home because of the extensive greenery.) The home was built by John V. McDonnell, an early day Tulsa oilman who came from the East to take advantage of the Cushing oil strike. He became interested in architecture and along with his partner, B. T. Nelson, designed many homes and commercial buildings in Tulsa. McDonnell enlisted the aid of Tulsa architect John Duncan Forsythe (Downtown Walk I) in the planning of his home. Finished in 1922, the home was patterned after sketches and photographs of his ancestral home in Carrie-Ma-Cross, north of Dublin, Ireland. McDonnell bought acres of walnut trees in

ALFRED AARONSON: Books and Art

Like his father, Alfred Aaronson was one of Tulsa's most important civic leaders. He not only spearheaded the drive for a new metropolitan library for Tulsa in the early 1960s but was largely responsible for Tulsa's acquisition of Thomas Gilcrease's collection housed at the Gilcrease Museum (Gilcrease Museum Walk). After learning that Tulsa was about to lose the Gilcrease collection, Aaronson and his wife launched a three-year effort to save the Institution, which resulted in the passage of a bond issue permitting the city to acquire the museum and its contents.

Osage county and used the wood extensively on the inside for beams, woodwork, and doors. Outside he used the walnut for the window ledges; the exposed exterior beams are oak. Between the beams is differently patterned brick-work around each window. Much of the window glass was salvaged from old New England homes and brought to Tulsa. The stone walls are eighteen inches thick. The home still has its original roof, which exemplifies the splendid quality of the materials and workmanship that went into its construction. The three layers of cypress shakes produce a thatched appearance, and the sloping roof line follows the eyebrow shape of the second story windows.

(Next door to the right (east) is a Spanish Colonial Revival. The home was designed in the early twenties by Reginald D. Johnson, a famous southern Californian architect, who built the Santa Barbara Biltmore Hotel.)

Turn left at 21st Street and walk toward the Skelly Mansion. Another home of note is on the next block, again across 21st Street, at **1029 East 21st Street**. The home was started in 1916 by Lionel E. Z. Aaronson for his son, Alfred E. Aaronson. Aaronson's home is characterized by its formal arrangement enriched with classical detail. Two Doric columns support the pedimented entry. The door is flanked by leaded glass windows with tracery. Balustrades are featured on the front porch and over the east wing and west porch. Over the windows are pronounced keystones, and dormer windows are on the third level. The rough textured limestone foundation is not typical of the Georgian style. Until recently, the only tree indigenous to the Maple Ridge neighborhood, a huge, two hundred-year-old oak tree called "The Shadows," shaded the home on the west.

As you return to your car parked on Madison Boulevard, think about Lionel Aaronson's advice to his son Alfred that he paraphrased from Ecclesiastes, "The name that one leaves behind him at death is better than the good oil that he was anointed with at birth"

S wan L ake

THE SWAN LAKE TOUR is characterized by distinctive shops and restaurants on the north and south with the history of Tulsa's 1920s preserved in between. Photographs of the era show men in straw hats rowing Gibson girls across the lake, and wild parties, overflowing from the International Petroleum Expositions (first held in 1923), are still vivid memories to long-time residents. Today it is one of Tulsa's most charming, older neighborhoods.

Park at Lincoln Plaza on Cherry Street on the northeast corner of 15th Street and Peoria Avenue. Walk through the parking lot to Quaker Street and turn left at 16th Street.

CHRIST THE KING. Walk one block to your first stop, **Christ The King Catholic Church.** A combination of Gothic and Byzantine architecture, the church, designed in 1927 by Chicago modernist Francis Barry Byrne, is an innovative work of liturgical architecture. Many people during the 1920s considered this art-deco styled church radical in design. Departing from the narrow or cross-shaped form of the traditional Catholic churches, Byrne, who believed that form followed function, facilitated the function of worship by creating an edifice that would stress the primacy of the Eucharistic altar. The effect of the strong vertical elements is to lift the eye heavenward aiding the architect's desire to raise his art from "merely decorative to a more spiritual, pedagogical purpose." Christ the King is the only Tulsa church mentioned in *American Churches* by Roger G. Kennedy of the Smithsonian Institute.

DISTANCE

1.5 miles

TIME

1.5 hours

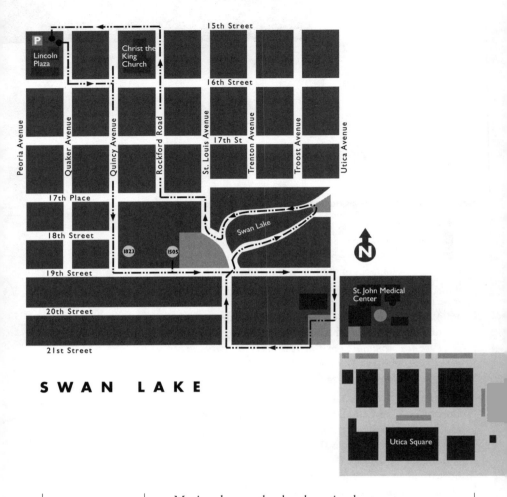

S W A N   L A K E

Moving closer to the church, notice the strong masonry masses terminating in delicate finials (spires) reflecting several influences. The crenelated brickwork creates a Byzantine effect, and repeated use of the pointed arch is a reworking of the Gothic motif by Bryne who was a contemporary of and, in fact, studied under Frank Lloyd Wright.

Byrne loved to work with brick, and the craftsmanship in this brickwork would be difficult if not impossible to reproduce today. The bricks run up at forty-five degree angles to produce spearlike bodies; the corners themselves are cambered (blunted at forth-five degree angles). Byrne explains the finials in his notes on the church:

Terra cotta was selected for the ornamental parts because, being a clay material, it was closely related to the brick; therefore, it unified with it. It also permitted a thing rarely done since the Renaissance, the actual reproduction of the sculptor's models in baked clay. Usually the architect makes a drawing of an ornament, a modeller (not an artist) reproduces it in clay, and the reproduction of that is then made and baked. The result is mechanical and lacks sensitivity. In this case, Mr. Iannelli, the sculptor, formed the actual designs into clay which were then baked, so that his artistic feeling, which is very great, was preserved in the finished product.

As you enter the church through the west doors, the concept of a congregation gathered around an altar is very evident. All eyes are directed toward the altar, even those belonging to the regal personages captured in the **stained glass windows**. These windows, done under the direction of Iannelli, are described in *Liturgical Arts* magazine as ranking "among the best to be found in the United States. . . . The figures are superb in color and design." The

GLORY OF LIGHT

The glory of Christ the King's windows is in the life and movement of light. From sunrise through midday to night, the colors change, each according to its particular nature, gaining or losing prominence like the instruments in an orchestra. The blues wax when the light wanes; the reds and yellows gain brilliancy at midday. Blue will spread and make the adjacent red appear purple; red spreads very little, orange and yellow, not at all. Through the day there is an ever-changing display of gem-like tones. The light reflects on the dark pews in a multicolored pattern, traveling over the course of morning Mass from the side altar to the main altar to highlight Christ the King.

Christ the King Church

SWAN LAKE: BEGINNINGS

The Swan Lake Addition is part of the original land grant from the United States to the Creek tribe in 1852, signed by President Millard Fillmore. The allotment of 800 acres to Samuel August Orcutt's Creek Indian wife and children encompassed this neighborhood. The Orcutt's home (no longer standing) was a three-story brick located at 16th Street and Peoria Avenue. Colonel Orcutt was a pioneer cattle rancher and a member of the first Oklahoma legislature. His wife, Adaline, was a native of Choska, a Creek village near Coweta, and was a trilingual Indian interpreter for Reverend Robert Loughridge, the first missionary to the Creek Nation. Her father, Alvin T. Hodge, owned much of the land upon which Tulsa stands.

south windows contain Biblical kings. Starting closest to the altar are the three wise men: Melchior, Balthasar, and Caspar (with a black face). The other two are David and Melchizedek, Old Testament kings. On the north wall are king/saints of the Christian era: St. Wenceslaus of Czechoslovakia, St. Henry of Bavaria, St. Stephen of Hungary, St. Edward the Confessor of England, and St. Louis of France. Their crowns are off in reverence to Christ the King, toward whom they are gazing.

Most of the iconography of the church is familiar; however, other details have to be pointed out or explained. Note the **ceiling**. White triangles cutting into the dark polished wood carry out the crown image of the windows, reiterating the theme for which the church was named.

The crown is again seen in the mosaic impaneled above the altar with Christ holding the orb of the world in His hand. Designed by Emil Frei, Inc. of St. Louis, the **mosaic** was made in Italy by the Ravenna Mosaic Company of New York.

The **main altar** is of limestone with a verde marble top. Deep horizontal flutings reinforce the verticality of Byrne's design. On each side of the front sanctuary behind the **Mary and Joseph Altars** (also designed by Ianelli), are mosaics designed by Bruce Goff, a Tulsa architect (Downtown Walk II). The torches and candleholders on the altars were designed by Byrne and made by the Empire Chandelier Company of Sand Springs. The art deco fixtures reflect the time period in which Byrne worked.

The fourteen **bas-relief sculptures** on either side of the room depict the stations of the cross. Beginning next to the Joseph Altar, the sculptures end with the deposition of Christ, beside the Mary Altar.

Returning to the entrance, reflect on the art, imagery, and design of the church, the first in the world to be dedicated with the name of Christ the King.

QUINCY AVENUE. Once outside, turn left and begin walking south on **Quincy Avenue**. The first block on Quincy Avenue contains homes that are excellent examples of the bungalow style. Comfortable porches with tapered posts or battered piers, rafters extending well beyond the walls, and gently pitched,

broad gables, occasionally with a second story and dormer windows in the roof are hallmarks of this design. Built by the thousands during the 1900 - 1940s, the bungalow is an American classic.

The next two blocks illustrate how bungalows, like other simple but functional houses, were subject to architectural variations—California, Colonial, and Tudor. Also mixed among the homes are quadraplexes and six-plexes of stone, clapboard, and stucco. The Swan Lake Area has more two-and-three-story 1920-1930 multi-family apartments and duplexes than any other residential area in Tulsa.

On the northeast corner of Quincy Avenue and 19th Street, the residence at **1823 South Quincy Avenue** is of Mediterranean influence translated to a contemporary design. H. William Schlingman, the original owner, was a German builder influenced by the Arts and Crafts Movement, with its emphasis on designing and detailing that harkens back to the old-world tradition. Schlingman's skill and individuality are evident in this home (visible in the front porch) and others he constructed in the area.

NINETEENTH STREET. Turn left (east) on 19th Street and walk to the red street sign, 19th Street. Turn left to view the

Bungalow house
with double gables

Schlingman, the original owner of the residence at 1823 South Quincy, was a German builder influenced by the Arts and Crafts Movement, with its emphasis on design and detail that harkens back to old-world traditions.

house at **1505 East 19th Street.** The mansion was built by Judge Spillars in 1924 on part of the three acres he purchased in 1922 for $12,000. The house is considered to be an adaptation of Georgian style which originated in England and was perpetuated on southern plantations. Spillers donated the land east of his home as an addition to Swan Lake Park, and as a buffer from development.

Return to the street and walk toward the stop sign at St. Louis Avenue. Instead of circling Swan Lake at this time, an optional tour, consisting of a quarter of a mile loop, is recommended. Continue to the end of 19th Street where it joins Utica Avenue. Look across Utica Avenue to **St. John Medical Center,** named after the only disciple who did not forsake Christ in the hour of His Passion.

The hospital's history began in the spring of 1914 when the citizens of Tulsa (population 25,000) realized the need for a large hospital with modern facili-

1823 South Quincy

ties. Doctors contacted the Sisters of the Sorrowful Mother, a community of nuns founded in Bavaria in 1883, who operated a hospital in Wichita, Kansas. The Sisters visited Tulsa, and then approached the Bishop of Oklahoma City for permission to start a hospital in his diocese. On February 14, 1926, Dr. C. D. F. O'Hern admitted Mrs. Charles Brown, and on that same day, she gave birth to a daughter—St. John's first baby. Today, all that is standing of the original structure is what was referred to as the "West Wing," the red brick building facing Utica Avenue.

UTICA. Turn right and walk south to the fountain in front of St John Utica Tower in **Helmerich Park.** The fountain sculpture, commissioned by Helmerich and Payne, is an aquamobile by New Orleans artist Lin Emery. The large work of art is a series of eighteen large mobile forms. The following remarks made by Emery originally made more sense because the structure moved.

"Motion is my prime concern. I want to evoke the essence of movement—flight, dance, gestures, pantomime. The forms arc through space, dipping and rising, sometimes skimming the surface of the water in the pool, sometimes swooping fifteen feet in the air."

Entitled *Free Enterprise,* the name is a play on words describing not only the intended random movement of the sculpture but also the business activity represented by F & M Bank. The aquamobile presented many challenging technological problems. For the desired color and weldability, the piece was constructed of a specially produced bronze alloy and stainless steel. In addition, the fountain was built to withstand Oklahoma's common sixty-mile-per-hour winds. With energy conservation in mind, the fountain is run by only two three-quarter horsepower pumps. The end result is a cool respite from the noisy streets inviting the viewer to pause and watch.

The nearby sculpture, portraying an average,

middle-aged man on a park bench reading The Tulsa Tribune, is *The Newspaper Reader* by J. Seward Johnson, Jr. It is typical of Johnson's artistic approach to place figurative works of art in unassuming natural settings. His work is represented through-out the United States including Houston, Los Angeles, Washington, D. C., and New York City. Take time to feel the different textures on the sculpture: the smoothness of his skin, the fabric of his tie, or the detail on the wing-tip shoes. The bronze reader is so realistically created that sitting next to him you can read the newspaper. The date of the edi-tion, December 19, 1981, is signifi-cant because W. H. Helmerich, Sr., in whose memory the art work is dedicated, passed away on that day. In describing the selection of the piece, W. H. Helmerich, III stated, "Since Dad loved the park we wanted something that would not only tie in but would also fit

Free Enterprise,
Helmerich Park

his tastes. Johnson's work is subtle and consistent with our fountain: it came to belong there."

W. H. Helmerich, Sr. was instrumental in the history of **Utica Square,** the shopping center across the street. His person-al involvement with the center is a tale told by merchants and patrons alike. Helmerich is reputed to have appeared unan-nounced in the Square on weekends, accompanied by a pair of trimming shears and a trash bag.

Unless you decide to take advantage of one of Utica Square's restaurants or shops, continue across the park to the building on the west.

Hidden away, just left (south) of this building, is a small enclosed park with benches providing a wonderful respite half way through the tour.

SWAN LAKE. Take the west exit from the enclosure and continue west along the sidewalk on 21st Street to St. Louis Avenue. Here, turn right (north) and walk a block to the lake. The placid scene of **Swan Lake** belies its raucous past. Around the turn of the century, Colonel Orcutt used it as a watering hole for his cattle herds, and because it was always an area of natural beauty, the lake (once quite a bit larger) attracted many visitors seeking a cool place to swim, picnic, or fish. As Orcutt's lake became more popular with hundreds of families streaming in on horseback or by buggy, he decided to create what became Tulsa's first recreational park.

Opening in 1907 (when Tulsa's population was an estimated 7,800 with 150 new families arriving every week to seek work in the Glenn Pool Oil Field), Orcutt's park had free admission, but boating, swimming, and amusement concessions required purchasing a ticket. The formal opening had the First Annual Log-Rolling of Woodsmen of the World. By 1910, a street car was bringing people the more than two-mile distance from downtown Tulsa to the park where the line

BUILDING UTICA SQUARE

When its first developers, Dale Carter and Don Nix, decided to build Utica Square, the investment was considered risky at best. The year was 1949 and suburban shopping malls were still in the future. With few exceptions, people went downtown to shop. The center was built in a series of small blocks, much like a village.

In 1963, Carter and Nix sold the Square to investor Bill Kistler. Also in 1963, a fire destroyed one of the major buildings, which contained a few shops and the Southwest's largest bowling alley. Kistler rebuilt an elegant structure (now housing Miss Jackson's, Petty's Fine Foods, and others) to attract quality merchants. Following his instincts, Helmerich initiated marketing changes which were viewed by many as unorthodox. "The first thing we did was plant trees—over three hundred of them to make the Square beautiful. It's the foliage and the

landscaping that make it so attractive and give it the little town atmosphere," says Helmerich. "You can park in front of the store and walk under the trees. It's exactly the opposite of a mall."

More of Helmerich's rationale influenced the direction of the center: "I knew that my wife never bought anything without going to every store in town—she'd go to Leisure Manor on Eighteenth Street, she'd go to Miss Jackson's downtown—she'd visit them all and then decide what she wanted. So we tried to convince all the better specialty stores that they should be in one location … it seemed to work, because in the next seven or eight years we got literally every good specialty shop in Tulsa.…We could give Petty's to Miss Jackson's and get five times the rent, but people in the area want a grocery store."

WATERFOWL SOCIETY

The Swan Lake Waterfowl Society was given conservation awards and recognition for its waterfowl project at Swan Lake. The society conducts annual spring training classes beginning in early April for volunteers and interpretative guides who give guided tours, with advance requests, of the lake's waterfowl. They also collect the eggs and help with projects on the lake. (Those interested in becoming a volunteer to help and learn about the lake, its history, wildlife, its identification of waterfowl and plants, or those with groups desiring tours can call 918-743-6878 or 918-585-5775 for details.)

ended. At various times the park featured a natatorium (covered swimming pool), an airdrome (open air dancing pavilion), moving picture show, balloon ascension events, and animal menageries. In 1911, Orcutt installed a forty-foot high, six-hundred-foot roller coaster costing $7,600. Because of the expansion of Tulsa toward the park, Orcutt sold his property to E. J. Brennan, who platted it as Swan Lake Addition.

Start your walk around the lake on the boardwalk, built over a marsh where waterfowl hide and nest. As you proceed counterclockwise, notice the homes built between 1918 and 1950, which represent a variety of architectural styles including Spanish, Georgian Revival, and vernacular interpretations honoring the swan. All sit on high ground overlooking the city-owned lake. A fountain, erected in 1937, graces the lake. Made of concrete resembling rock, it is a scenic attraction with its cascades of water. Particularly in winter, with its showering falls frozen, the fountain takes on a magical quality.

The lake is a sanctuary for waterfowl and other aquatic life, and its most impressive inhabitants are the Trumpeter Swans, the largest and rarest of the world's eight species of swans. Grace and beauty of figure, the long arched and flexible neck, the elevated wings, and its buoyancy and skill in turning and gliding over the surface, all contribute to the ornamental effect of the swan. Unlike the fussy geese and ducks (the swan is actually a sub-family of the duck), there is a calmness and dignity about the behavior of swans which has always excited admiration and has caused these birds to figure in much poetic literature. Poets, incorrectly, attributed great musical ability to their song of death, and the pair of North American Trumpeters possess a powerful and sonorous voice, like that of musical trumpets. These great vocal powers are due to the coiling of the greatly elongated trachea within the sternum.

The lake's preserve contains 32 species of native North American waterfowl, ducks, geese, and the swans. The birds that live on the lake throughout the year were purchased from licensed waterfowl breeders by money from public donations and from donations made by the Swan Lake Waterfowl Society. There are about 100 birds in the permanent collection, but

Canada geese, left,
and wood duck

from November through early March, the lake is the temporary
home for more than 200 migrating ducks. The Waterfowl collection is a continuing project of the Swan Lake Waterfowl
Society, and the Tulsa Park Department provides the maintenance of the park and lake.

The mallard is the most common wild duck on the lake
(most domestic ducks are its descendents); the male has a green
head, a white band around the neck, and a red breast. Wood
Ducks are another very colorful resident here, (the males have a
green and white crest, reddish bill, eyes, and breast). There are
also pintails with long pointed tail feathers; shovelers with large
spatula or spoon-like bills. Redhead and Canvasback ducks are
somewhat similar in appearance with their reddish heads and
grayish-white bodies on the males. Both are excellent diving
ducks. The Ruddy duck, not commonly seen as often, except in
wild areas, are here; the males have a bright blue bill, white
cheeks, and a ruddy colored body in the breeding season. The
only non-native bird to North America that lives at the lake is
the Mandarin Duck from Asia. The male has bright orange
plumage on his face and on the erect wing sail feathers. The
most comical water bird on the lake is the coot, sometimes
called the "mudhen." This small chicken-like bird is all black
with a whitish bill, and a very short tail.

Canada, Lesser Snow geese, White-Fronted and Emperor
geese join the parade along with the least terns, birds on the
endangered list who fly from Arkansas to feed on the small min-
nows in late spring and summer.

Swan Lake is an excellent site for photographing birds.
Usually very fleeting and elusive, here the birds are easy to view.

*Swan lake's
preserve
contains 32
species of
native North
American
waterfowl,
ducks, geese,
and the swans.*

THE BEAUTIFUL SWAN

Swans mate for life, but will generally accept a new mate when death becomes to one of the pair. They are fierce protectors of their young. Look for cygnets (baby swans) to appear on Swan Lake in late June or early July. Although a few species of waterfowl on the lake are free-winged, the pair of swans has one wing clipped as well as the majority of the birds in the permanent collection of waterfowl. This is to keep them from leaving and for their protection from being harmed if they were to fly out.

The swan has, from a very early date, been protected by legal and regal order. In England during Henry VII's reign, the theft of a mute swan's egg was deemed an offense punishable by a year's imprisonment, and the theft of a swan itself a serious crime.

ST. LOUIS AND SEVENTEENTH. After circling the lake, turn right (north) on **St. Louis Avenue** and walk toward 17th Place. Once in this area a dairy farm produced milk for residents if they would come and get it. So different from the sterilized cartons in the supermarket today, personalized service such as this has gone the way of the streetcar which dead-ended on St. Louis. The ambience of the era is alive, however, in the homes, with their different architectural mixes and crafted detailing. On 17th Place, turn left (west) and then right (north) on what used to be Jasmine Street and now is **Rockford Avenue**. The New England atmosphere is enhanced by a white picket fence and tree-lined streets.

If you are interested in antiques, walk to 15th Street and stroll between Peoria and Utica Avenues. Browsers will be delighted with the offerings of the shops and restaurants.

Return to **Lincoln Plaza** on Cherry Street. The plaza began life as Lincoln Elementary School, built outside the city limits in 1909, only two years after statehood. The continuing growth explosion of the era had necessitated the voting of a bond issue, and its success resulted in construction of Bellview (Lincoln) Public School. Two of the more famous alumni of Lincoln Elementary School are William "Hopalong Cassidy" Boyd and Tony Randall.

Take time to explore the brewery, relax, and enjoy the outdoor dining at several of the restaurants with spectacular views of downtown.

Brookside

THE STORY OF BROOKSIDE begins with Tulsa's oldest historic roots—paralleling the time of the Council Oak Tree (Riverview Walk). Change is a hallmark of this enduring neighborhood, a center of continual growth and activity from 1848 until the present. Its proximity to downtown and ritzier neighbors sustains Brookside as a thriving area today. In the past, this same proximity to the Lochapoka ceremonial village and to the river made it a desirable location for ranching activity, which was monopolized by one important Creek Indian family, the Perrymans. Ironically, this ever-changing neighborhood embraces the most continually inhabited unchanging tract of land in Tulsa—Zink park and the Perryman cemetery.

To begin the tour, turn south on Trenton Avenue off 31st Street and park along the east side of Zink Park. Picnic facilities are located here, and restaurants are along the walk route.

PERRYMAN CEMETERY. Walk east on 32nd Street a long block (almost to Utica Avenue) until you see, surprisingly, tombstones on your left. This **graveyard** is one of the few unchanged historical sites in Tulsa and all that remains of the great Perryman ranch, which once encompassed more than 60,000 acres between Tulsa and Broken Arrow. At least forty graves of the Perrymans and other Native Americans are in this 150-foot square tract of land. The cemetery also contains Civil War soldiers, buried in their blankets, and settlers with no burial plots of their own. The number of children buried here evidences the hard life during pioneer days in Oklahoma; one half

The first Perryman home, on what is now 41st Street between Utica and Peoria Avenues, was Tulsa's first post office, operated at first by the Pony Express.

DISTANCE
1.5 miles

TIME
1 hour for walking plus time for shopping and eating

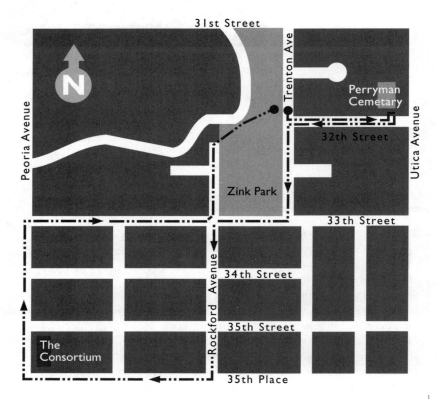

B R O O K S I D E

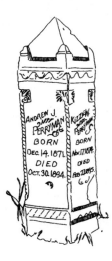

of the graves are for children who died between six months and five years. Most of the others were under forty when they died.

In 1848, Lewis Perryman arrived in this area to establish a trading post along the river, after a cholera plague had forced his family to leave Broken Arrow. (His father Benjamin Perryman, born in Georgia in 1755, had traveled the Trail of Tears to Oklahoma; in 1836 at Ft. Gibson, George Catlin painted Perryman's portrait, now hanging in Smithsonian Institution.) Life for the Lewis Perrymans was interrupted when the Civil War passed over and around Tulsa, scattering the Lochapokas (Riverview Walk) and other Creeks loyal to the Northern cause. Most went to Kansas, and the Perrymans left their comfortable log home to join the trek. Many starved; others were made helpless from frozen limbs. Infants died and were buried in the snow. The Union Army was unprepared for the responsibility of furnishing food, clothing, and shelter for the thousands who slowly collected on the Verdigris River in Kansas. Lewis, one of many who froze to death in camp, was buried in an unmarked grave in December, 1862.

In the graveyard, the heart-shaped tombstone belongs to one of Lewis's sons, George Perryman, who returned from wartime exile to find his home overgrown with weeds and underbrush, fences broken, and livestock gone. George, equal to the task ahead, managed the ranch with such industry and sound business sense that he eventually became the largest landholder and cattle king in the Creek Nation. He held over 200,000 acres under lease from the government through his brother, Legus, chief of the Creek Nation and one of the two chiefs buried here. (The first of George's homes, the "White House," is marked by a historical marker at 41st Street between Utica and Peoria Avenues. Located at this address and operated at first by the Pony Express was Tulsa's first post office.)

Rachel, George's wife, died on February 7, 1933, and is buried in this cemetery near her husband. At their home the family kept open house for the countryside, and sheltered Native American orphans and the homeless. It is said that at one time twenty-three unrelated children as well as kinsmen were cared for in the Perryman home. At a later time, because Rachel wished to live closer to the new mission school in Tulsa, George built a larger home on "High Hill" at Sixth and Main Streets. Later, when selling this home for $60,000, Rachel would not accept a check. Gold was brought from St. Louis, and Mr. J. H. McBirney (Riverview Walk) delivered the payment and acted as interpreter to Mrs. Perryman, who still spoke mostly Creek. Outliving all of her family except one son and a daughter, Rachel sold much of the land for residential use and became a wealthy woman. Still it was difficult to persuade her to give up her horse and buggy and ride in her chauffeured Packard.

After reading the tombstones, backtrack to the park and turn left (south) on Trenton Avenue. Turn right on 33rd Street. Walk west, bearing in mind how the land might have looked when Lewis Perryman first came here. Proceed to **Rockford**

EVERYTHING OLD IS NEW AGAIN

Paradoxically, the Brookside shopping area is one of the oldest, yet newest shopping districts in the city. Tulsans remember it as an alternative to downtown shopping, with the merchants stressing casual dress for their customers. (There was even a Short's Day Parade.) Today, the area is a paradise for browsers and epicureans with antique shops, galleries, and restaurants. The Consortium, a partly enclosed mall, "specializes in ambience."

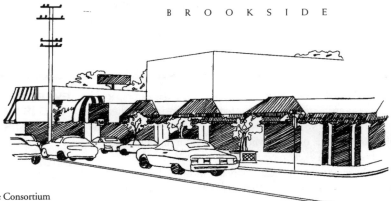

The Consortium

JOHN ZINK

Zink Park's namesake, philanthropist John Zink, hauled 1,500 tons of boulders from his ranch in Osage County for the park — these giant boulders stacked like building blocks are great fun for children. The thirteen-acre park, given to the city by Zink in 1942, now contains a lively playground with a sprinkler pool and lighted tennis courts.

Avenue. This area is thought to be the location of Lewis Perryman's 1848 settlement, an enormous one-and-one-half-story house of hewn logs, with great stone fireplaces, outbuildings, and slave quarters — an extensive establishment for the three or four wives, children, and slaves of a man of large influence, a man who raised and sold cattle and traded with the remote Creek outpost, Tulsey, and passing Osage Indians.

At Rockford Avenue turn left (south) and continue three blocks to **35th Place.** Turn right (west) at the stop sign. You may have noticed along the walk the bells of Southminster Presbyterian Church calling attention to the hour of the day. The tintinnabulation, especially wonderful at noon and five o'clock, rings out familiar hymns. As you pass the first block and cross Quincy Avenue, begin noticing the houses on the south. They are typical of early bungalow style, and during the spring in particular reflect the owner's pride and joy in gardening.

CONSORTIUM. On **Peoria Avenue** turn right (north) at what is now a Tulsa renaissance shopping area. North of the **Consortium,** are other places to shop and eat. You also might enjoy investigating the opposite side of the street as Brookside is changing every day with galleries, restaurants, and one-of-a-kind shopping.

ZINK PARK. At 33rd Street, turn right (east) and walk two blocks to Zink Park. At the corner of the park (Rockford Avenue), turn left (north) down a shady lane. At the lane's end cut through the park toward the trees. You will find an opening with a rock path, surrounded in spring with azaleas. A bit farther is a peaceful and secluded area hidden from the traffic of Peoria. Continue east through the trees. Your car is just over the hill.

Woodward Park

ON THIS WALK you will visit the ornamental gardens of Woodward Park, pass through the Garden Center, a fashionable home of early Tulsa, and stroll along Terwilleger Boulevard, where you can view some of the elegant, older homes of the neighborhood. Fall and spring are the best times to catch most of the flora and foliage at their peak, but a snowy winter walk through the park is breathtaking. Summer is a good time to view the many varieties of annuals, but walks during the early mornings or at twilight are recommended to avoid the summer heat.

WOODWARD. When first proposed as a park, Woodward Park, Tulsa's most popular horticultural attraction, was originally considered too far out in the country. In 1909 the isolated tract of land, once known as Perryman's Pasture and accessible only by wagon trails, was acquired by the city for a park site. Many early Tulsans thought the city's action was foolish and the $100-per-acre price outrageous; the area was so far outside the city limits it hardly seemed plausible that it would one day become a valuable asset.

The park later became a subject of litigation in the Oklahoma Supreme Court. Earlier the land had been part of a 160-acre allotment given to Helen Woodward by the Five Civilized Tribes Indian Commission. In 1909, Helen was only fourteen when her father, Herbert E. Woodward, acting as her guardian, sold the land to the city. Sixteen years later Helen (Mrs. S. H. Slemp) decided to test the purchase of the land in court because she had never given her consent for the sale.

DISTANCE

1 mile

TIME

1 hour

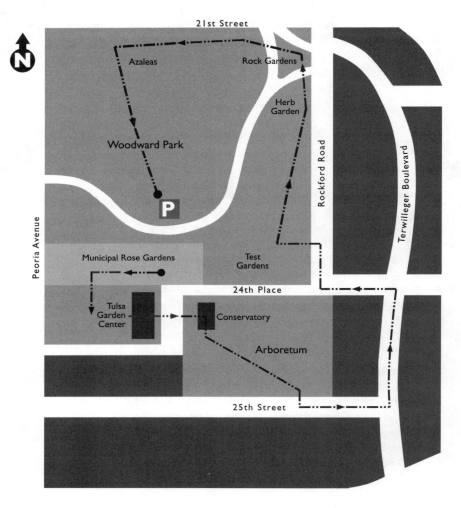

W O O D W A R D   P A R K   A R E A

After four years of litigation, Mrs. Slemp lost her case to the city.

Today, the 40-acre park boasts a wide variety of horticultural delights including rock gardens, an old English herb garden, a terraced Italian Renaissance rose garden, a Victorian conservatory, a three-acre arboretum, an azalea garden displaying 15,000 azaleas, and 35,000 daffodils naturalized for early spring bloom. The park provides many swing sets, benches for resting, and open areas for picnicking or playing outdoor games. In snowy weather the main drive, which slopes downhill to the west, is closed to traffic so people can sled. In addition, Woodward Park, sometimes referred to as Songbird Sanctuary, is a haven for birdwatchers.

For this tour park in the lot adjacent to the Municipal Rose Gardens, on the south side of the park.

ROSE GARDENS. Begin your walk near the central pool of the **Municipal Rose Gardens.** In 1937, only two years after the first plantings, Better Homes and Gardens Magazine presented a bronze plaque to the Tulsa Garden Club. The award was quite an achievement. Since then the Rose Garden has continued to receive the highest praise. Noted English rosarian Harry Wheatcraft pronounced it the finest in design and maintenance that he had seen in the United States, and the garden, also, was featured in the 1961 edition of *Great Gardens of America.*

The six terraces of Italian Renaissance influence start at the top of a gentle slope and end 900 feet later at Peoria Avenue. Stone steps connect the terraces, separated by English-ivy-covered rock walls. Pools, some with small fountains, are featured on all levels, and cone-shaped junipers are planted in the lawn areas and near the terrace walls. Clipped hedges of either Hall's honeysuckle, euonymous, abelia, Buford holly, or dwarf Chinese horn holly are maintained above each wall. Southern magnolia trees, deciduous holly, and mugo pines are included in the gardens; on the southern boundary are junipers, Austrian and Scotch pines; on the east is a screen of Arizona cypress, arborvitae, and junipers, providing a backdrop to the trellised roses.

Presently there are about 9,000 rose plants representing some 250 varieties in the rose gardens. The roses bloom from

WOODWARD PARK

LOCATION: Southeast corner of 21st Street and Peoria Avenue.

HOURS: 5 a.m. to 11 p.m. every day, free of charge.

GARDEN CENTER

LOCATION: Adjacent to the rose gardens at 2435 South Peoria Avenue. Plenty of free parking is available behind the Garden Center.

HOURS: Weekdays, 9 to 4, free of charge.

SHOP: The Center's Gallery of Gifts sells garden-related items.

EVENTS: Frequent lectures, classes, shows, and sales. The Tulsa Audubon Society meets the third Tuesday of each month, September through May, 7:30 p.m. at the Garden Center. For more information on specific dates and times, call **(918) 746-5125.**

THE ROSE

The Queen of the Flowers' long history of cultivation began 5,000 years ago in China. Roses became so popular during the Han dynasty, land needed for agriculture was tied up in rose gardens, threatening food production. During ancient Greek and Roman times, love and beauty became synonymous with roses in their association with Aphrodite and Venus. Later, the white rose became a symbol of the Virgin Mary's purity, and the briar rose was said to have sprung from Christ's blood as he wore the crown of thorns. According to 19th-century etiquette books, the Victorian gentleman, speaking the "language of flowers," gave a single red rose to signify "I love you"; a return gift of a red rose sent by the lady sealed the match. A single yellow rose implied fickleness; a white rosebud said, "I am too young to love"; a single rose leaf meant, "I care not."

May until frost (usually the latter part of October), but the peak bloom periods are mid-May and mid-October. The showiest bloom period is in spring; the color and duration of the blooms, however, last longer during fall. The most popular variety of rose is the hybrid tea, offering an exceptional range of color, fragrance, flower size, and shape for bouquets and for bright display in the garden. The floribunda rose lives up to its Latin name, "flowers in abundance," for with ordinary care it will blossom continuously from early summer until frost. Colors cover a gamut of hues, from snowy white to sparkling yellow to deep tones of crimson. Grandifloras are the result of an attempt to create a novel type of rose that would have both the beautiful blossoms and long stems of the hybrid teas and the hardiness and flower clusters of the floribunda. The most successful attempt thus far is the Queen Elizabeth, located west of the central pool, to the right (north) of the central path, on the main terrace.

As you wind your way down through the terraced rose gardens, take time to enjoy the beauty of the massive plantings of labeled roses. Subtle fragrances reminiscent of tea, nuts, fruit, spices, or honey can be detected from many of the roses.

TULSA GARDEN CENTER. When you reach the bottom level, walk under the cedar trees to your left to the front lawn of the **Tulsa Garden Center.** The lawn is beautifully landscaped with plantings of dogwoods, whitebuds, and Japanese maples flanking a small fountain with benches. From the fountain you have a good view of the Garden Center. The house is a typical 1920's version Italian villa with a loggia (arched passageway) and French doors. The red-tiled roof and symmetrical design with classical influences evident in the fluted Ionic columns suggest an Italian Renaissance source for the home, a very popular revival style of the time (Philbrook Museum of Art Walk). The twenty-one-room home was designed by Tulsa architect Noble B. Fleming and completed in 1919 for David Travis, who had recently arrived in Tulsa from Pennsylvania. The home next door was built for his brother and is still a private residence. The Travis home changed owners several times—the Arthur J. Hull and George Snedden families.

(Cleora Butler, in her book *Cleora's Kitchens: The Memoir of a Cook & Eight Decades of Great American Food,* published in 1985, aptly describes Mrs. Snedden's delight at moving into the home in 1932 after the Hulls decided to sell because of financial reversals during the Depression. Published by Council Oak Books, Ltd., Tulsa, Oklahoma, Butler, through stories, menus, and recipes, recreates her own remarkable history—and Tulsa's.)

The home was later purchased by the city in 1954 for $85,000 from the W. G. Skelly family, who owned the villa but did not live in it.

Walk around the back of the home to enter the Garden Center. Inside the Center in the appropriate rooms are photographs showing the home as it was furnished by the Travis family. Visit some of these rooms that still retain the craftsmanship and charm of the original home. The extensive wood carvings were created by Italian workmen, and the former library, which is downstairs, has one of the few gold leaf ceilings in Tulsa. Proceed upstairs. The large oil painting on the stair landing was a gift of the Snedden children to honor their father and mother. (The painting hung in the same location when the house was owned by the Sneddens.)

On the second floor is the **Garden Center Library,** one of the finest horticultural libraries in this part of the country. It offers approximately 6,000 volumes on floriculture, landscaping, wild flowers, flower arranging, and many other related subjects. Anyone can use the library, and members can check out books. Be sure to visit the yellow marble bathroom (one of ten), which is on the south side of the library.

CONSERVATORY. Walk out the back of the Garden Center to the **Woodward Park Conservatory.** Originally constructed in 1924-26, the conservatory was recently restored to its classic Lord and Burnham style. Mrs. Snedden used it exclusively for orchids. Now the conservatory is used by the city park's department for its colorful seasonal displays of plantings. In addition, the conservatory houses a collection of exotic plants from the major rain forest regions of the world and permanent collections of succulents and many cacti varieties.

Presently there are about 9,000 rose plants representing some 250 varieties in the rose gardens. The roses bloom from May until frost (usually the latter part of October), but the peak bloom periods are mid-May and mid-October.

Woodward Park
Conservatory

In front of the conservatory is a sunken garden, whose color and design is rotated to reflect the seasons. In spring, Coronation Gold pansies and pink larkspurs or foxglove abound; in summer, a fleur-de-lis pattern is created with three plantings of Joseph's coat surrounded by copperleafs, lantana, and marigolds, all encircling a pond of water lilies; fall plantings include flowering kale and cabbage. (Over 80,000 plants for the Woodward Park area and all other city owned parks, including Gilcrease Museum, are grown in the greenhouses behind the conservatory.)

TULSA ARBORETUM. From the sunken garden pass through the parking lot, which was once a swimming pool, to the **Tulsa Arboretum.** In 1964 the city set aside three acres of land to grow trees that do well in the Tulsa area. Many of these trees were donated in the name of a person or an organization. Look for your favorite trees and spend some time enjoying the beauty and peaceful surroundings. Benches are placed throughout the park for resting, and if lucky, you might come upon a lone flutist or guitar player. Look for the redbuds in mid-March and the dogwoods in mid-April. Toward the end of October the sugar maples and oaks (especially the scarlet) begin to display their brilliant hues. The arboretum also includes a beech tree and ginkgo tree, both uncommon to Tulsa.

Continue along the path to **25th Street.** At the exit look to your right to see a row of young Caddo sugar maples, planted to replace elm trees that once lined the street. The maples from Red Rock State Park near Caddo Canyon are native to Oklahoma and were propagated in the park's greenhouses.

TERWILLEGER BOULEVARD. Turn left at the arboretum exit, walk a short distance to **Terwilleger Boulevard,** and turn left again. Named after Claude H. Terwilleger who developed the area, the street was once much wider to accommodate the median with horse trails down the center. This block features many differently styled homes built during the twenties. Spanish and English Tudor influences are common to the area. Beginning the development of Terwilleger Heights in the early twenties, Terwilleger sold over $200,000 worth of lots in the first week.

DISPLAY GARDENS. At 24th Place turn left; then turn right on Rockford Avenue. Walk through the first opening in the fence on your left to the **Iris Display Garden** where 217 varieties are grown. Keep walking until you reach the **All American Rose Selections Test Gardens,** one of twenty-two sites in the United States used to test and to evaluate roses grown in different areas of the country. After two years of evaluation, roses with the highest scores throughout the country are named All American and introduced to the public bearing the label AARS. The value of a discovery such as a new color is so great (royalties may bring the grower millions of dollars) that rose breeding has been surrounded by an aura of romance and adventure.

The Peace rose was almost prevented from developing by World War II; a cutting from a sturdy plant with pale gold blossoms was aboard the last American plane out of France in November, 1940. Not until five years later did rose breeder Francis Meillant learn that his exported cuttings had been used to propagate the rose that many experts consider the best ever

ANNE HATHAWAY HERB GARDEN

Started about fifty-five years ago by Jewel Huffman, the garden is fully maintained by the city horticultural staff. They start 3,000 plants from seeds and cuttings in the park's greenhouses; they water, care for, then transplant the herbs to the garden in April. The labeled herb garden exhibits some forty-two different herbs, including scented geraniums, different sages, basil, lemon thyme, burnett, rosemary, marjoram, oregano, and tarragon. The herbs grow from May until frost, but the best time to experience the garden is during the summer after a rainfall. You are encouraged only to pinch off a leaf to smell and taste.

Shakespeare Fountain

developed. (The Peace rose is on the upper terrace of the Rose Garden. It is next to the steps to the next lower terrace, to your right as you descend.)

From Test Gardens walk up the stone steps and continue north, paralleling Rockford Avenue until you reach the **Anne Hathaway Herb Garden**, named after Shakespeare's wife. After circling the garden, follow the path north across the drive to the upper rock garden. Two rock gardens (the lower garden continues on the west side of the drive) were laid out in 1930. Honeycombed limestones were hauled from northeast of the city and were placed in a naturalistic manner. A watercourse was designed to give the effect of a chain of lakes and streams and a number of small springs although they all originate from the city's water supply. Constructed of reinforced concrete, the watercourse was then covered with rocks, soil, and plants so that the cement work might not be detected. Water flows from the initial springs and pools at the head of the upper garden and trickles over the rocks and down the ravine, terminating in a bog garden. Rock pathways, benches, and foot bridges

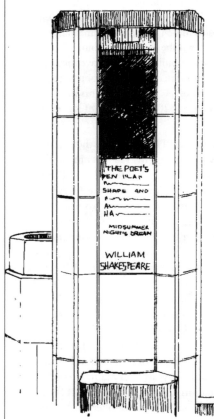

were devised to help visitors enjoy the walk; luxuriant shade from the many native oaks and hickories invites walkers to tarry.

The focal point of the upper garden is a fountain and pool with a bronze Cupid and a dolphin spray surrounded by a nymph and two statues of Pan at the rear of the main pool. A constant succession of flowers bloom during the seasons, beginning with 6,000 yellow, white, and blue pansies and 5,000 tulips in the spring. At the end of April the flowers are removed, and the entire area is planted with salvia, coleus, begonia, copperleaf, periwinkle, impatiens, and airplane plants. In October yellow, white, and red container-grown chrysanthemums are sunk into the beds.

Walk across the drive to the **lower rock gardens,** featuring more than 15,000 azaleas. Walk down to the first lagoon onto the **observation bridge,** constructed of concrete made to resemble logs and stumps. From here you can view a small pond filled with goldfish; originally it contained tropical water lilies, a number of which were furnished by Waite Phillips (Philbrook Museum of Art Walk).

After leaving the overlook, walk back up the hill to the path and take the right fork until you reach a concrete monument with a bronze **bas-relief of Shakespeare.** It was designed by Adah Robinson (Downtown Walk II) in 1932 as a drinking fountain. Notice the intricate filigree detailing, featuring characters from *Midsummer Night's Dream.* (Directly north of the fountain are two redbuds; to their east is a good-sized native smoke tree.) Continue west on the main path through the aza-

JEWEL OF THE PARK

Planted during the late sixties and early seventies, the azaleas converted a badly eroded hillside into "the jewel of the park." Beginning in April, thousands of red, white, pink, purple, and orange blossoms display their dazzling colors along with the many redbuds and white dogwoods in the area. The best time to see the azaleas is mid-April, but be prepared for crowds of people.

leas to a small, pink memorial stone, on the right side of the path, dedicated to Lilah D. Lindsey, a descendent of the Perryman family (Brookside Walk) and the first woman to serve on the school board. Behind the stone, an oak tree grows at an angle because it was originally one of a pair.

Follow the path and take the middle fork to the bog garden; cross the bridge to view the sculpture, *Appeal to the Great Spirit,* by Cyrus E. Dallin. Installed in the park in 1985, the 1907 sculpture, based on the original that is in Boston, stood in Central High School as a "symbol of excellence in academic life." As you make your way back to your car, think of the saying inscribed on this plaque. "O great spirit at thy call we have pledged our youth ever climbing, one and all, seek eternal truth."

River Parks

STANDING ON THE BANKS of the Arkansas River in the fall of 1832, Washington Irving, who was touring the prairies, wrote: "[The river] presented a broad and rapid stream, bordered by a beach of fine sand, overgrown with willows and cottonwood trees. Beyond the river, the eye wandered over a beautiful champaign country, of flower-plains and sloping uplands, diversified by groves and clumps of trees, and long screens of woodland; the whole wearing the aspect of complete, and even ornamental cultivation, instead of native wildness."

The river on its journey through Tulsa has not always enjoyed such a favorable response. Full of sand bars and sandy water, the broad river bears little resemblance to itself at its point of origin: Beginning in Leadville, Colorado as a snow-fed, fast running, clear mountain stream, the river twists and turns through four states before it empties into the Mississippi River.

For the early Creek Indians and white settlers in the new town of Tulsey, getting across the Arkansas River was slow, wet, and unpredictable. Before the bridges were built, people and cattle either waded across or took unreliable ferry boats. The 1895 Frisco Railroad bridge was the first permanent structure built to break the river's barrier. Then in 1904, three Tulsans privately financed the first wagon bridge at Eleventh Street. Their plaque said, "You Said We Couldn't Do It, But We Did!"

Practically everything that has happened to the river since has faced opposition and skepticism. The river's undrinkable,

DISTANCE

7 miles of trails

salty water was at one time called "the nation's largest open sewer ditch." During talk of turning the river into a navigable waterway, Will Rogers quipped, "Paving the Arkansas would be cheaper than making it navigable."

The river's unpredictable waters flooded Tulsa fifty times between 1907 and 1961. The Great Flood of May 20, 1943, left more than four thousand people homeless, destroyed over four hundred homes, and killed twenty-one people.

More recently, the Keystone Dam, built upstream in 1964, enabled the river to become a valuable resource, providing not only a link between the east and west sides but a pleasurable setting for outdoor activities. With the completion of the low water dam in 1983, the dream that had been imagined for

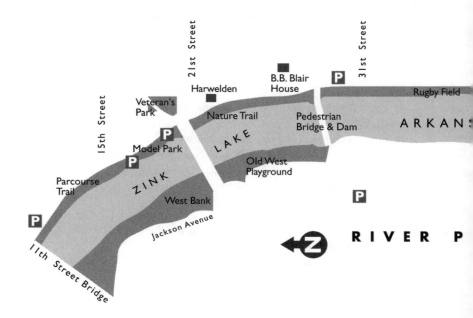

decades of creating an urban lake was fulfilled.

Today with its cultivated improvements, River Parks, nestled on the banks of the Arkansas River, recalls Washington Irving's description. Seven miles of landscaped linear park land on the east bank and two miles on the west bank offer the jogger, bicyclist, nature lover, and family a wealth of resources. Within walking distance of downtown, it is a gathering place for the people of Tulsa and the

RIVER PARK EVENTS

The park is the center of more than 20 special events each year, including movies, concerts, races, and festivals:

Easter Egg Hunt at the River West Festival Park

Summer Movies starting in May; July 4th

Fireworks Display and live entertainment at dusk on both banks of the river

Sandcastle Contest in July at the 61st Street and Riverside Drive sand bar

Riverfest on Labor Day weekend with music, crafts and food

Symphony at Sunset in September

Oktoberfest, a German Festival of authentic foods, arts and crafts, music, and dance the third weekend in October on the west bank

Tulsa Run, a fifteen-kilometer race.

Christmas Lights the Park, usually the first Sunday in December at the Pedestrian Bridge

Amateur rugby games Many Saturdays 1 to 5, September through November and March through May. A schedule is posted on the bleachers or call 743-1043.

For exact dates, check local newspapers or call The River Parks Authority at 596-2001.

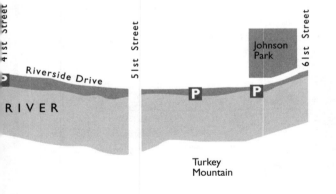

RIVER PARKS

LOCATION: Along Riverside Drive on the east bank between 11th and 81st Streets and on the west bank between 11th and 31st Streets.

FACILITIES: Accessible from either side of the river.

PARKING: Available near the major areas of activity (See map) .

Sand castles at River Parks

third most used park in the city, attracting over 800,000 people annually.

Future plans for the River Parks system include a pedestrian/bicycle pathway over the 71st Street bridge to connect with Turkey Mountain. To the south the trail will eventually tie in with the Creek Turnpike trail and connect to the Jenks Pedestrian Bridge. To the north the trail will continue underneath the 11th Street Bridge and connect with the Tulsa/Sand Springs trail. By the year 2000 one will be able to walk or ride a bicycle from Highway 97 in Sand Springs south to 101st Street in Tulsa, east to Memorial Drive, with no red lights.

Today, each section of the river's edge offers a unique experience for the walker. Plenty of benches are strategically located along the river for resting, picnicking, or viewing the river and its people. Spring and fall are wonderful seasons to catch the beauty of the foliage surrounding the river, and the sun's rays reflecting on the water during the evening hours of summer can be spectacular. Regardless of the season, decide how far you want to walk (including the return to your car) and what you want to see and do; then pick the area and park in the lot closest to your walk. (For the benefit of those for whom distance

holds some significance, trail markers are every half-mile on the east bank.)

Turkey Mountain, across the river, can be reached from the east side by taking the 71st Street Bridge to West Tulsa; turn north on Elwood Avenue and continue until Elwood turns into 61st Street. From the west side, exit east at 61st Street from the Okmulgee Bee Line and continue until 61st Street turns into Elwood Avenue. The parking lot is adjacent to the area.

EAST SIDE OF THE RIVER. Starting at the south end of River Parks near 59th Street is Jingle's View Overlook, a quiet place to observe nature, such as eagles, offering exciting panoramic views of downtown and of Turkey Mountain. Especially beautiful in the fall, Turkey Mountain, on the west bank of the river, is a 147-acre wilderness area acquired in 1978 by the River Parks Authority. This rugged, heavily wooded property contains unmarked hiking trails. A swath of wilderness in an urban setting, it has been allowed to return to its natural state. Wild turkeys, once prevalent in the area, have been reintroduced. Oak trees native to Oklahoma, including bur, post, and blackjack, are abundant on the mountain. Other trees include black hickories and, near the water, cottonwoods, sycamores, and black willows. (Although Turkey Mountain looks temptingly close across the river, it must be reached by car.)

Near 56th Street is the site of the annual Sandcastle Contest. The sand bar is a good place to play in the sand.

More trees can be viewed in the vicinity of the **51st Street Bridge.** Look for the Osage-orange (hedge) trees. Their rough-textured fruit, three to five inches in diameter, is just perfect for throwing. Salt cedars, reaching only ten to fifteen feet in height, grow in the sandy area. In summer they produce masses of small, very beautiful pink flowers. The trees, which extract their water from great depths, were introduced to this country from Asia. Also found nearby is the Kentucky coffee tree, which can grow up to one hundred feet in height. During the Civil War era, its beans were often used by pioneers to make coffee because of the South American embargo.

The widest land mass along the water's edge is around **41st**

TREES TO LOOK FOR

Trees to look for on the trail are the red mulberry and, along the river's edge, cottonwoods and black willows. The trumpetvine, which displays its showy orange flowers from the middle of summer till frost, and the Virginia creeper, with its brilliant red leaves in fall, can be found on many of the trees in the area. The Carolina snailseed, recognized by its ruby red fruit, blooms in late summer and fall. Scattered along the trail throughout the park, the numerous redbuds are especially beautiful in spring.

Street. The area contains a children's playground, a rustic gazebo, a picnic pavilion, and restrooms. Situated among a grove of red mulberry trees is a frisbee golf course of eighteen baskets, and farther north near 36th Street is a rugby field, home of the Tulsa Rugby Club.

A scene of major activity is the **31st Street area.** Here you can see fishermen near the dam catching striped bass. Also in the area are bicyclists, roller skaters, and strollers enjoying the many amenities. With its covered walkway, the **Pedestrian Bridge** is a converted, old railroad bridge spanning one-quarter mile over the river. The walkway was partially funded by *The Tulsa Tribune*'s promotion that sold inches of the bridge for $5.50 per inch. The bridge now serves as a link between the east and west bank trail systems. (If you wish to walk across the pedestrian bridge, information about the west bank trails is included at the end of this walk.) The bridge includes several overlooks, offering views downstream to the south—including Turkey Mountain—and upstream toward downtown. Below the bridge, waterfall effects are created by the multi-leveled fountain and dam; the eight-foot high dam produces the two-mile **Zink Lake**, which offers water recreational opportunities for rowing and canoeing. The Sooner Rowing Association has a club house on the west bank at the River west Festival Park, a departure point for sculling activities on the lake. The focal point of the dam area is **Blair Fountain,** named after the late Tulsa oilman B. B. Blair, who was connected with Waite Phillips's oil operations. Blair's southern-styled home and expansive front lawn, directly across Riverside Drive, reflect his boyhood background - his father, Walter Blair, captained a steamboat and owned a packet line in the upper Mississippi Valley.

Across Riverside Drive you can see the back of **Harwelden.** On the north side of the **21st Street Bridge** is the **Model Park,** one of the most popular areas in the park system.

trumpetvine

Beautifully landscaped, the area includes a shelter with restrooms, drinking fountain, and picnic tables. A river overlook is used for fishing or watching the river. Also in the area is a playground featuring a fort and other newly designed play equipment for children. Nearby, *The Web,* a contemporary cube sculpture was created by Tulsa artist Ann Tomlins. The theme of the sculpture is the relationship of technological and ecological systems.

Scattered throughout the Model Park are barbecue grills, benches, and picnic tables available on a first come, first served basis. Outdoor lighting permits park use until the 11 p.m. curfew. Everything in this area is fully accessible to the handicapped.

WEST SIDE OF THE RIVER. At this point on your walk, you might wish to walk across to the west side of the river on the 11th Street Bridge, which features a separate lane for pedestrian/bicycle traffic protected by a concrete safety barrier. From the bridge you have a good view to the south of the islands created by dredging, slated to become a wild life habitat for waterfowl. Willows and cattails are currently being introduced to these islands.

Two miles of lighted jogging paths between the **11th Street Bridge** and the 31st Street Pedestrian Bridge now traverse what once was a devastated dumping ground. Given a massive facelift in the late 1970s, the banks were sculpted, an eight hundred-foot **marina** was formed, topsoil was laid, and over one thousand trees were planted. Later, part of the land between 11th and 21st Streets was sold to help finance the low water dam. The remaining two-mile stretch of park land hosts a variety of seasonal activities.

From the west bank, you have an ethereal view of Tulsa as the skyline emerges from a fringe of trees. The reddish brick building south of downtown isolated in greenery is the Sophian Plaza (Riverview Walk). In addition to scenic views, the west bank also has the added advantage of being far removed from the traffic noises of Riverside Drive.

Farther south is the new **Festival Site** featuring a two thousand-seat amphitheater and floating stage, restrooms, picnic

HARWELDEN

LOCATION: 2210 South Main Street.

HOURS: Monday through Friday, 8:30 to 4:30. Rented for parties and weddings (call 584-3333).

HISTORY: The thirty-room English Gothic Tudor mansion was built in 1923 for oil millionaire Earl Palmer Harwell. In 1967, Mrs. Harwell deeded her home to the Arts and Humanities Council, an advocate of artistic endeavors in Tulsa and producers of the Harwelden Institute, (an aesthetic workshop for teachers), an artists in schools program that annually reaches 150,000 children, and the Tulsa Chautauqua. If you visit Harwelden, be sure to look for the rose and thistle motifs throughout the home. They are visible in its carved wood paneling, plaster ceilings, and stained glass windows.

View from the West Bank

areas, concessions, and a special concrete pad for tennis and volleyball.

A small-sized "ghost" village in the form of an **Old West Playground** includes a stagecoach, opera house, and blacksmith shop tailored to accommodate children. Picnic tables, barbecue grills, benches, a drinking fountain, and landscaping enhance the playground area.

Stretching out into the river is an expansive sand bar accessible from the west bank.

Adjacent to the Pedestrian Bridge is a small, landscaped concrete overlook, which takes you to the river's edge.

The River Parks is constantly in a state of change as new facilities are added and more trees and shrubbery are planted to make this green belt a popular and unique area in Tulsa.

Mohawk

WITH 2,800 ACRES of wooded park land, Mohawk Park is one of the oldest and largest municipal parks in the nation. (San Francisco and Philadelphia both have larger parks; Central Park in New York City is 840 acres.) Mohawk Park hosts many popular events and features a zoo (Zoo Walk), nature preserve (Oxley Walk), golf course, bridle trails, hiking trails, and a polo field. Choose an event or activity from the wide array the park offers and discover Tulsa's favorite resource for family recreation.

Events annually scheduled at Mohawk Park include Mohawk Open Trail Rides (monthly), the Zebco Fishing Derby (early June), Play Fair (June), Tulsa Pow Wow (July), and concerts. Check dates for individual events by calling 596-7855 or 596-7859. For park information and to reserve picnic shelters call 669-6272.

Mohawk Park is easily reached by taking Harvard, Yale, or Sheridan Avenues north to 36th Street North or by taking the 36th Street North Exit from Highway 75. You can ride a bus to the park: call 584-6421 for schedules and cost information. A $1.00 parking fee is charged seasonally on weekends and holidays to the park area. A mounted patrol protects the park during the warm months.

ZOO WALK. The Tulsa Zoo has evolved as an institution with a three-fold purpose: Conservation, Recreation, Education and Research. These goals are manifested in imaginative exhibits displaying animals in naturalistic environments.

Adults, who in the past have developed a state of boredom

DISTANCE

1 mile

TIME

2 hours

IT'S ALL HAPPENING AT THE ZOO

HOURS: 10 a.m. to 5 p.m. every day except Christmas and the third Friday in June. Visitors may stay on the grounds until 6 p.m.

ADMISSION: Adults, $4.02; Senior citizens, $3.02; children (ages 5-11), $2.01; children 4 years and younger, enter free. ($35-Family Memberships that allow free entrance and other benefits are available at the entrance.) Group discount rates, birthday parties, and after-hours picnic arrangements are available by calling 669-6600.

ZOO TRAIN TICKETS: Round trip adult tickets for the zoo train are $1.50; one-way is $1.00.

TOURS: Contact the zoo's Education Department at 669-6219 for Docent guided zoo tours.

CONVENIENCES: For your convenience, strollers are available for rental ($2 per day; wagons are $3) courtesy wheelchairs are available at the admissions office on a first-come, first-served basis.

ZOODAYS

SUNSET SAFARI: A reduced-admission event ($1.00 for everyone above the age of four) in July and August every Tuesday and Friday nights from 5 to 8 p.m.

ZOOLIGHFUL: A nighttime holiday light spectacular, displaying over 160,000 lights with an animal theme.

CHRISTMAS: During the Christmas season, except the 24th and 25th, from December 8-30th, from 6-8:30 p.m.; admission is $3.00.

HALLOWZOOEEN: A trick-or-treat trail through the zoo is October 28-30th, 6-8:30 p.m.; admission is $3.00.

staring through coldly functional bars, are now the most fascinated zoo visitors. In fact, you don't need a child as an excuse to visit the Tulsa Zoo. The Zoo offers adults a delightful opportunity to don their wildest evening apparel for a night among the animals with WALTZ On the Wild Side . . . a Black Tie Safari. The WALTZ is held on the third Friday in June each year.

Throughout the zoo you will see an insignia used to indicate vanishing species. Zoos have become the Noah's Arks of the 20th Century. They are often the last refuge many animals have against extinction. Information displays throughout the Zoo stress that extinction is forever. This sad commentary is never more poignant than while looking at an animal whose continued existence is in jeopardy. Some visitors are surprised to learn that the Tulsa Zoo is an accredited museum in addition to being one of the best zoos in this region of the country.

The zoo uses the most unobtrusive barriers possible between man and beast. Therefore, adults must be cautioned not to lift a child over a fence or rail, negating its purpose. As zoo personnel will attest, all of the inhabitants of the zoo are wild, and the sea lions and prairie dogs are not above nibbling at fingers. All of the zoo's animals (even the ducks and geese in the pond) are on special diets and are not to be fed by visitors.

For this walk the cooler seasons of fall through spring are preferable to the crowds and heat of the Oklahoma summer.

At the zoo's Safari Grille Restaurant, visitors may choose from a varied menu, including everything from cotton candy and corn dogs to grilled chicken sandwiches, salads, and other menu items which are added seasonally. Satellite concession stands operate throughout the zoo on a seasonal basis. Visitors may also bring their own picnics and use the zoo's ample picnic areas where they can relax and enjoy the animals. Private picnics and parties for groups from 2 to 2,000 or more can be arranged at the zoo after regular hours.

After entering the zoo, you will find information (to your left) on feeding times and new animal exhibits. The sea lions are fed during a daily demonstration at 2:00 p.m. Here you have a choice to make, either to start out your zoo walk on foot or take the easy way around with a one-and-a-quarter- mile train ride. Save this treat for later when it will be fully appreciated. Keep in mind the most valuable zoo suggestion—stop and read the labels.

The first stop on your Zoo tour is the **Chimpanzee Connection.** This facility, completed in 1991, has been acclaimed by internationally known wildlife researcher, Dr. Jane Goodall, as

Zoos have become the Noah's Arks of the 20th Century. They are often the last refuge many animals have against extinction. Information displays throughout the Zoo stress that extinction is forever.

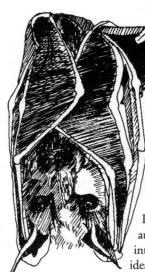

Bat in The Cave

being one of the best chimpanzee exhibits in the United States for both the mental and physical well-being of the chimps. Only glass separates visitors from the active chimpanzee family.

After leaving the building, walk on the boardwalk to view their island habitat. As the chimps entertain you with their comical antics, you might be reminded that they are man's closest relatives; the Academic *American Encyclopedia* claims that our DNA is 99% the same. Although it may be tempting to toss something to the chimps, this is strictly prohibited.

Next, follow the sign toward the Robert J. LaFortune North American Living Museum. Zoo authorities boast that the Tulsa Zoo was the first to introduce the Living Museum concept in a zoo. The idea of displaying living animals, plants, and native cultures together in a unifying theme has become widely adopted by many other zoos.

Your tour through the complex begins with the **Arctic Tundra,** continues with **Southwest Desert** and **Eastern Forest,** where an example of the artistry involved in such projects is recreated by a cave, where visitors can walk among stalactites and stalagmites and learn about the many different types of rock formations as well as what kinds of animals can be found in caves, including blind cave fish and salamanders. You will finish in the **Southern Lowlands** that houses a new 20,000-gallon shark tank, a renovated coral reef, and pelican exhibit.

Exiting from the Southern Lowlands, be sure to look for the siamangs. During warm weather, they are to the left of the path on an island in the duck pond. (In winter they are in the Main Building.) These apes have extremely long arms, which enable them to swing from branch to branch with incredible ease. Their placement on this island allows the viewer to enjoy their grace and beauty surrounded by a natural barrier.

Next is the **Children's Zoo.** Playground equipment in this area gives the children a chance to imitate the animals while adults seek out the benches and picnic tables. The barnyard is an area where visitors can come in contact with some of the residents here.

Before continuing farther, you might want to energize at the **Safari Grill**, a great addition to the zoo.

In the **Main Zoo Building** you will find a variety of animals, including exotic birds, reptiles, fish, and primates or monkeys. Many of these animals will move to the new Tropical American Rain Forest when it is completed in 1997.

After you leave this building, stop and enjoy the sea lions. Flanking their home are (to the left) the great cats, including Siberian tigers, African lions, and the highly endangered Snow Leopard from the mountains of Asia, and (to the right) the bears. Look for the large brown bears, and watch the antics of the spectacled bears as they climb the branches of trees placed in their exhibit.

If you are growing weary—abject fatigue with small children—you will enjoy a ride on the zoo train to the entrance. Riders get a narrated tour and a view of the zoo that those traveling by foot can never see. As you pass the African Savanna exhibit, keep your eyes open for zebra, kudu, gazelles, and giraffes.

Ardent walkers will prefer to continue on to the **Wetlands** exhibit where you can walk out on the boardwalk and see what animals have arrived to take advantage of this rich and diverse area. Nearby are Aldabra Giant Tortoises. You can get up close to these gentle giants when zoo personnel are available.

You are now nearing the end of your Zoo walk with one exciting exhibit left to enjoy, the **Elephant Encounter.** This new exhibit not only houses the zoo's elephants but offers visitors an opportunity to develop a real appreciation for these magnificent creatures. Some highlights of this outstanding facility are a life-sized diorama depicting a full-scale hunt scene of a Columbian era woolly mammoth by Clovis hunters, an interactive computer, which shows the differences between African and Asian elephants, and a robotic elephant's trunk.

Before leaving the zoo, pause to end your visit in the **Spotted Zebra Gift Shop**, where you will find something spe-

OXLEY TRAILS

TRAIL LENGTH: Six miles.

HOURS: The Oxley Nature Trails are open year round 8 to 5. The building is open 10 to 4:40 daily and Sunday 12 to 4:30.

FEES: On Saturday, Sunday, and holidays, there is a $1 parking fee at Mohawk. (A $1 enrollment fee is charged for classes, but you are mailed a free pass for parking.)

TOURS: Any group (six or more people) can book a guided tour by one of the staff members. **Call 669-6644 for information.**

A naturalist leading the group is the ideal way of enjoying the trails. Advertised through Oxley's newsletter and in local papers these special programs are often filled the day they are announced. Even though the trails are only approximately a mile in length, a staff member suggests one and one half hours is not too much time for the experience.

EVENTS: A Fall Festival may include "birding," edible wild foods, and live animal shows, among others.

NEWSLETTER: If you visit Oxley and become hooked on the adventure, make arrangements to be put on the newsletter mailing list.

TIMING YOUR VISIT: The best touring begins around September 15th and continues until the heat and bugs take over sometime in June. Early morning and evening are the best times for sightings of wildlife, but as the weather turns cooler many animals become more active during the day. If you enjoy a wintry walk, Oxley is wonderful in January and February. Ask about their winter trail guide brochure.

cial to remind you of your wonderful day and your renewed appreciation and respect for the animal world.

OXLEY NATURE CENTER WALK. Oxley Nature Center is an 800-acre wildlife refuge and nature preserve and, for some, this city's best kept secret. The purpose of the center is to provide a look at our land, water, and wildlife as they existed before we came.

The idea to establish a nature center in Mohawk Park began in 1975 with a group of citizens presenting their proposal to the Tulsa Parks and Recreation Board. Because the city did not have funds to pursue the project, the group organized to seek funding for the building of a facility on designated land in the park. In 1977, John T. and Mary K. Oxley, inspired by their love for the outdoors and pleas-

Redheaded woodpecker

ant memories of their courtship on horseback in Mohawk Park, initially donated $200,000 for this project. The Oxleys' generous donation inspired the present name of the facility, Mary K. Oxley Nature Center.

Oxley Nature Center is mentioned in *Where to Find Birds West of the Mississippi*. Over two hundred species of birds have been sighted in the area. Seven different species of woodpeckers reside here including the red-headed woodpecker, the Nature Center's symbol. The Harris sparrow can be spotted in winter along with various waterfowl such as the great blue heron, and in summer, indigo buntings, tanagers, and scissortail flycatchers. Wild flowers are beautiful in the spring and summer, and from mid-October Virginia Creeper and sumac add brilliant color. Also, the gift shop at the Nature Center deserves a visit.

OXLEY TRAILS Your first introduction will be the **Nature Center Building.** On entering the building, financed completely by donations, you will find interesting and educational displays which, using the center's philosophy of sensory awareness, cleverly involve the visitor as a participant. Be sure to investigate the weather station upstairs. Using the center's information, you can make your own forecast. However, remember that displays are not the focus of the center and are intended as only an introduction to the real, ever-changing display outside the building.

The brochures produced by Oxley's staff are free of charge. Even the novice will enjoy identifying wild flowers illustrated in two leaflets, *Spring* and *Summer*. Two others provide information on *Oxley Animals* and *Skyhunters*. These valuable tools assure full sensitivity and enjoyment while hiking on your own. The brochures of two trails, Red Fox and Blue Heron, help you hike at your own pace.

There are ten trails, covering over six miles, but most of the trails are short loops of a half mile or less. Begin your tour at the **Interpretive Building.** From here you can access most of the trail system easily. **Red Fox and Blue Heron trails** are accessible to wheelchairs, and their accompanying brochures are available in Braille. The brochures for these two trails are very entertaining and educational for both adults and children. Various sensory awareness activities will open another dimension to your

Oxley Nature Center is mentioned in WHERE TO FIND BIRDS WEST OF THE MISSISSIPPI. *Over two hundred species of birds have been sighted in the area. Seven different species of woodpeckers reside here including the red-headed woodpecker, the Nature Center's symbol.*

Dogtooth violet, coreopsis, green dragon, clasping-leaved coneflower

experience and you will become more intimate with life in the forest.

No printed trail guides are available for the remaining hikes, so armed with your wild flower pamphlet and the Oxley animal information, you are ready for the other eight trails. Named for the wild flower, **Green Dragon Trail** follows **Coal Creek**. **Prairie Trail** winds among prairie plants and wildlife trails of the old field area.

A boardwalk reaches to the middle of the marsh on **Blackbird Marsh Trail**. The **Wildlife Study Area** is part of an old field now being reclaimed and planted with wildlife food. **Bird Creek** runs through the wooded section, and on this trail, with proper timing, chances are good that you will spot an owl.

The **North Woods** is approached from a completely different parking area which is a half-mile walk from the trail head. It is the oldest part of the nature center and the least disturbed. The distance around the loop is approximately 6,000 feet, and from the parking area this constitutes a two mile walk. Three hours is the suggested time for this trail.

Beaver Lodge Trail is a site of beaver activity on **Mallard Lake**. **Sierra Club Trail** circles **Nelson's Oxbow**, home for many water animals and birds.

A parting word—no poisonous snakes have been identified at Oxley.

Redbud Valley

"**A**N ECOSYSTEM PAR EXCELLENCE" is one naturalist's description of Redbud Valley. Seen solely as a
natural unit, Redbud Valley is remarkable; seen in
relation to recent city growth, it is amazing. Apart from the
highly interesting scientific aspects, beauty alone recommends
this preserve as a premier spring and autumn walk.

Dr. Harriet Barclay, late Professor Emeritus of Botany at
the University of Tulsa, arranged for the area to be a project of
the Nature Conservancy in 1969. In 1990, the Nature
Conservancy transferred title of the property to Oxley Nature
Center, which now manages the site.

Autumn and spring, as with most nature hikes, are the best
times for the tour, but all seasons offer something of interest.
Autumn, particularly from the middle of October through the
first days of November, provides a glorious display of leaves. In
spring, the color and fragrance of redbud, hawthorn, Mexican
plum, spicebush, and smoke tree delight the senses, and the
wild flowers burst through the rich remains of last autumn.
(Because of the wide variety of flowering plants here, a wild
flower guide is almost a necessity.)

The trail at Redbud Valley is approximately one mile long.
Because of the terrain, the hike is mildly strenuous, and the
footing can be tricky in spots after a rain. Wear your outdoor
gear and sturdy shoes.

Be Aware: The tarantulas and scorpions are not a problem;
their sting is just painful. However, copperheads are sometimes
seen on the property. The area can have ticks in mid-summer,
and precautions to avoid them are recommended. The upper,

DISTANCE

1 mile

TIME

1 hour

REDBUD VALLEY

HOURS: The Redbud Valley Nature Preserve is open Wednesday through Sunday from 8 to 5. Closed Mondays, Tuesdays, and holidays. Please do not enter the area when the gates are closed.

LOCATION: To reach the preserve, proceed east from Tulsa on I-44, and take the 161st East Avenue exit. You must make two left turns, then a right to connect with 161st E. Avenue. Go north on 161st E. Ave. for approximately 3.8 miles to the preserve entrance, which is on your left.

FURTHER INFORMATION: For information about these, or general information on the area, contact Oxley Nature Center at **669-6644.**

exposed areas can be very hot in mid-summer. Take water and pace yourself if the temperature is above 90 degrees.

After you park, you can find trail information on the big sign on the west edge of the parking lot. You may want to stop by the **Visitor Center** (hours 11 to 3) before you begin the walk. The newly opened center has an increasing number of displays about the area, and you may visit with the naturalist and pick up brochures on the plants, birds, and fossils of the area. There are picnic tables and restrooms available here.

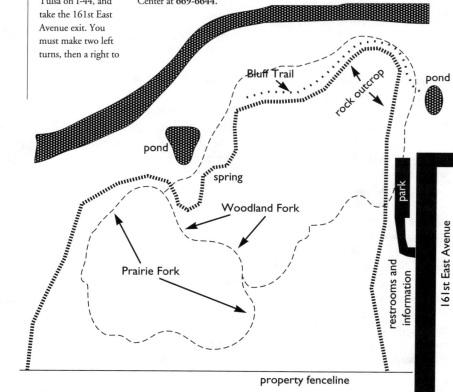

Bird Creek

Bluff Trail

rock outcrop

pond

pond

spring

Woodland Fork

Prairie Fork

park

restrooms and information

161st East Avenue

property fenceline

The trail begins at the west edge of the parking lot. Just a few yards down the trail you will come to a large yellow sign listing some do's and don'ts for your visit. Please read the sign, and follow the rules. They are enforced to ensure the preservation of this unique natural resource. The observant visitor will notice that those who have been here before have left the area clean and unaltered, and will want to preserve that tradition.

TRAIL. The trail begins under the sign that reads "Main Trail Starts Here." Here you start by climbing rather steeply up the hillside. As you ascend note the large limestone slump blocks that have broken off the hillside above and for millions of years have inched their way downward. They are covered with lichens, some large and showy, and at least three kinds of fern. In spring, these boulders will be covered with blossoming columbine, beautiful in the spring with their red flowers. This is your first indication of the special character of this area, as Columbine is a flower of the Ozarks, and is very rare this far west.

At the top of the grade, the trail will level out, although the presence of the limestone rocks just under the soil makes the trail surface uneven. Take a moment to look closely at the **limestone.** Much of it will be riddled with holes and cavities, known as "vugs." This indicates that the limestone was formed as part of an ancient coral reef, similar to what one would find today in the Bahamas. Common trees in this area include chinquapin oak and green ash.

As the trail proceeds, you will begin to notice that the trees become smaller and open areas appear. The soil layer on top of the limestone is becoming too thin to support trees, and

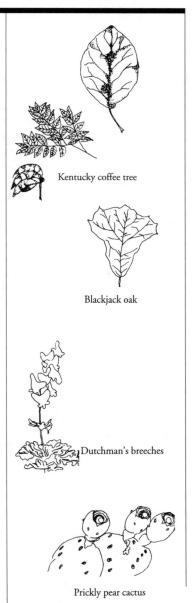

Kentucky coffee tree

Blackjack oak

Dutchman's breeches

Prickly pear cactus

Although the ice never got this far south, it did descend into central Kansas, and the habitat here was much cooler and more moist than now. As the ice retreated and the climate here warmed, the sugar maples disappeared, except for a few which managed to hang on in the sheltered, north-facing valleys of this special preserve.

other plants increase in frequency. Look along the trail edge for the first appearance of **prickly pear cactus,** which is common in the drier areas. This section of the trail will have an abundance of wild flowers, especially in late summer and early fall. Don't be disturbed if you see signs of fire in this part of the preserve. The Nature Center staff has undertaken a management plan to preserve the open, grassy areas on the preserve, and prevent the invasion of woody species into the area. A part of this management plan involves controlled burns to remove the unwanted species, so the fires are a benefit to the plants and wildlife of this section.

Soon the trail will enter the forest again, and you will come to a sign and fork in the trail. The right fork (marked **Woodland Fork**) continues through the woods, gradually descending until you come to the next intersection at the top of the Ravine. The left fork, signed **Prairie Fork**, is a slightly longer path that passes through an open grassland. Whichever fork you take, you will end up at the same spot, the top of the Ravine. First time visitors are urged to take the Prairie Fork to experience the full range of habitats on the preserve.

Prairie Fork trail crosses an area with much Prickly Pear cactus. However, the sharp-eyed visitor may find another cactus species here, Missouri Mammalaria. This is a low growing clumping cactus, and can be difficult to spot beneath the grasses and wild flowers. This part of the preserve is very dry and hot in summer. Consequently, it provides good homes for tarantulas and scorpions, which burrow in under the rocks.

The trail soon approaches the edge of the limestone bluff, where **Bird Creek** has cut down through the rocks. The first spot where the trail comes to the edge is called "**The Edge of the World**" by the preserve staff. The view to the northwest from here is breathtaking, especially when the leaves are off the trees. You can see for miles across the shallow valley formed by Bird Creek.

The trail turns right at this point, but before proceeding too far, take a moment to look for two interesting tree species. Growing up from below the bluff you will find sugar maples. These are leftovers from the last ice age, some ten thousand years ago. Also found in this area are several specimens of smoketree, an uncommon tree in Oklahoma. Named for its springtime blossoms with little hairs of greyish color which give its smoky or hazy appearance, the tree is also found in Chandler Park. It thrives in these two places because of the well-drained, shallow limestone soil.

At the next intersection, the trail to the left descends steeply through the **ravine.** Before you start down the narrow defile, take a deep breath; you'll need it to "ooh and aah" at the beauty before you. Dropping from the top of the limestone layer, the trail takes you to the base of the cliffs formed by the erosion of Bird Creek. This beautiful area is the most striking natural area anywhere near Tulsa. Along the cliffs are formations of rocks that seem to be melting or dripping in appearance. This is a precursor to the stalactite or stalagmite (the one from the ground contains a "g") formation caused by the evaporation of drip-ping water having a high lime con-tent. While walking under the overhang, one can't help speculat-ing the consequences of the mas-sive formation's deciding today is the day to release its hold on the shale underneath.

Climbing the ravine

The trail will take you across **two bridges** at the base of the cliff. The first bridge marks the opening of a large cave. If you have a light you may want to explore a short way into the cave, but please do so carefully, and enter only between April and October. There are **bats** in the caves, and they must not be disturbed during the cold months of the year, when it is important that they preserve their energy supplies.

The next bridge crosses the

Man's encroachment on nature that ultimately determines his own survival is too familiar to require further documentation here. However, one is all the more thankful to have this slice of an American wilderness left untouched to teach some of the secrets of nature's aging process—and how amazing that this sanctuary is only twelve miles from downtown Tulsa.

water emerging from a spring. The **travertine spring** is natural; travertine is a light-colored limestone formed as a deposit of limy springs. Following the stream to its source; you see that it emerges from the rocks and is fed by seepage from the plateau above. In spring, or during rainy periods, the water may emerge from the bluff with surprising force. When the weather has been dry, the flow from the spring will slow to a trickle. Consequently, the pond below may be either full or almost dry.

Before leaving this beautiful area, look carefully for **ferns** growing in moist places. Seven types of fern have been identified here. One is called "walking fern," a rare species that proliferates when the tip of one frond bends and touches the ground, producing another fern.

Now the trail descends the slope, winding around more limestone blocks. Soon you will be at the bottom of the hill and the trail will turn east. The habitat here is more typical of Oklahoma river bottoms, but the slope on your right still has a few surprises. In very early spring, this hillside may be rich with the pink-white blooms of Dutchman's-breeches, another Ozarkian wild flower. Among the rarest plants in Redbud Valley, the flower is named because of the pantaloon appearance of the blossoms which cling in vertical rows to a slender stem. An untrained eye might pass over it, and clumsy feet might step on it; however, once pointed out, one flower directs the way to another until the hillside is alive with these tiny, delicate, pink and white flowers. In fall, the uncommon blue ash tree may be found by looking for its peculiar yellow leaves.

The trail eventually turns away from Bird Creek, and begins a gentle climb that will take you across the hillside and back to the parking lot.

Man's encroachment on nature that ultimately determines his own survival is too familiar to require further documentation here. However, one is all the more thankful to have this slice of an American wilderness left untouched to teach some of the secrets of nature's aging process—and how amazing that this sanctuary is only twelve miles from downtown Tulsa.

Philbrook

A LTHOUGH VILLA PHILBROOK exhibits many features reminiscent of an Italian villa, it actually combines characteristics of several styles. Echoing the grandeur and elegance of the past, Philbrook announced Waite Phillips's twentieth-century wealth. In 1925 when he started his home, Phillips had sold his independent oil company for $25 million in cash. The mansion, completed in 1927 at a total cost of $ 500,000, demonstrated Phillips's admiration for the Italian Renaissance villas he and his wife, Genevieve, had discovered while touring Europe.

In the year of the villa's completion, the Phillipses gave "the grandest party of the era" to celebrate their new home. Trucks bursting with flowers began arriving at dawn for a sit-down dinner for five hundred, and that night when Genevieve made her dramatic entrance down the stairs, all the guests cheered. The evening reportedly cost well over $20,000. (Novelist Edna Ferber, an early houseguest, wrote in a national publication that the villa was a $2,000,000 mansion fitted with gold-plated faucets. Her ridiculing tone of newly-rich oilmen is said to have made Waite Phillips physically ill for days.)

Friends say the Phillipses built the villa as a place where their two children could entertain friends; Helen Jane was sixteen and Elliott was ten at the time. Waite, however, was not content just to enjoy his wealth; he found fun in hunting the dollar, not in possessing it, and he continually looked to see where it might be needed. After only eleven years of living in Philbrook, Waite donated his home to be used as an art museum, saying, "All things should be put to their best possible use."

Rarely has a villa built in the 20th century come closer in architecture and landscaping to the style of a Florentine villa of the 15th century. . . . Through a blend of elective affinity, good taste, and remarkable architectural skills, Edward Buehler Delk conceived a home of such gracious proportions and of such organic unity that it has nothing to envy beside its prototypes in the hills of Florence.

CORINNA DEL GRECO LOBNER

TIME

2 hours

WAITE PHILLIPS

Waite Phillips's success, like that of many other Tulsans, came from oil. He often told his friends that he was born with no particular talent or anything akin to genius. In 1925 during his announcement of retirement at age forty-four with a net worth of $40 million, he commented, "I've just been lucky." Tulsa banker J. J. McGraw (Maple Ridge Walk I) believed the success was more than luck; he said, "It was due to good judgement in choice of men for his organization and a keen appreciation of real oil values. He isn't a gambler. He is a shrewd investor. I don't want to say he's the best oil man on earth . . . but I have never seen a better."

Waite's childhood provides no clues to his later success. As teenagers he and his twin, Wiate, left their modest home in Iowa to backpack through the Rocky Mountains and along the Pacific coast. After Wiate's death from a ruptured appendix, Waite returned home at age nineteen. Later he joined his brothers Frank and L. E. in their oil business in Bartlesville, but after eight years he felt compelled to venture out on his own. As Waite's son, Elliott, later explained, "If two men are riding the same trail, one has to be in front." Soon afterward Frank developed the Phillips Petroleum Company, and Waite established an oil company in Tulsa in 1918.

Today Philbrook Museum of Art offers a chance to view art works in the intimate and charming atmosphere of a villa graced by beautifully maintained formal and informal gardens. Many of the rooms on the first floor of the villa retain their original aura, especially the **Great Hall** and staircases, the **Library, the Music Room**, and the living room—now the **Italian Room**. Other rooms were altered to create gallery space.

In 1990 Philbrook opened a **new wing**, a 70,000 square-foot expansion, that allowed the original villa to be dedicated entirely to its permanent collection. The new **rotunda entrance** leads to all of the museum's major functions—the **museum shop**, the **Helmerich Gallery** of temporary exhibitions, the **auditorium**, the **library**, the **museum school**, the staff offices and storage facilities, the **restaurant**, and the **permanent collection in the villa**.

The art collection at Philbrook spans many centuries and represents many areas of the world. Its Native American collection reflects the wishes of Waite Phillips, who said, "Oil fortunes were made out of the Indian lands. I have a deep feeling of gratitude to the American Indian and I want to see his culture preserved." Some outstanding works to look for are the black pueblo pottery made by world-famous Maria Martinez of San Ildefonso and the best known and probably the most perfect basket made by the celebrated artist Datsolalee. The site of the Indian Annual Exhibition for many years, Philbrook also has an extensive collection of Native American paintings.

Another outstanding collection includes the Samuel H. Kress Foundation gift of thirty-nine Italian paintings and pieces of sculpture dating from the fourteenth through the eighteenth centuries. Kress (1863 - 1955), founder of the S. H. Kress & Co. variety store chain, assembled a vast collection of paintings, sculpture, decorative arts, and drawings by European masters. The bulk of Kress's works was given to the National Gallery of Art in Washington, D. C. Believing that works in storage were of little use, the foundation determined to donate the remainder of the collection to museums and universities where the art works might have a profound effect. Moreover, when feasible, cities that had Kress stores were selected so that the people who patronized them were those who derived the most benefit. Philbrook Museum of Art was

East Terrace view, Philbrook

among the initial eighteen public museums and twenty universities selected as recipients for the loan in 1953 and as a gift in 1961. To complement the style of the house and grounds, Italian works were designated for Philbrook.

Other collection areas represented at the museum include African masks and ritual objects; Asian rare porcelains, ancient ceramic tomb figurines, cricket cages, snuff bottles, and other works in ivory, jade, and other media spanning 3,000 years; and American, English, and French paintings from the seventeenth through the twentieth centuries. Because the collections are changed periodically, check at the desk for current installations. Also, inquire about special traveling exhibitions.

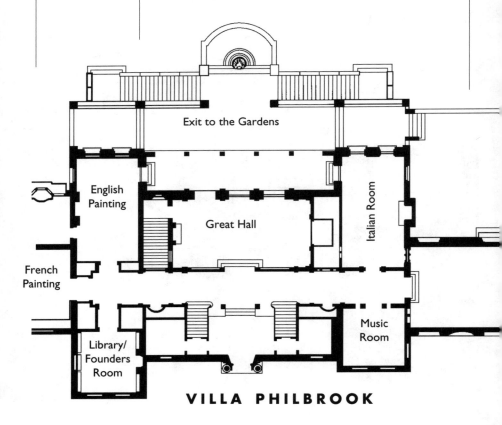

Exit to the Gardens

English Painting

Great Hall

Italian Room

French Painting

Library/ Founders Room

Music Room

VILLA PHILBROOK

ENTRANCE. To begin your walk , go past the new entrance of the museum to the former doorway of the villa. Here you are transported to the grandeur of Tulsa's oil boom days by Philbrook's massive Italianate presence. You might detect a glint on the stucco facade from the sun's rays.

NEW WING

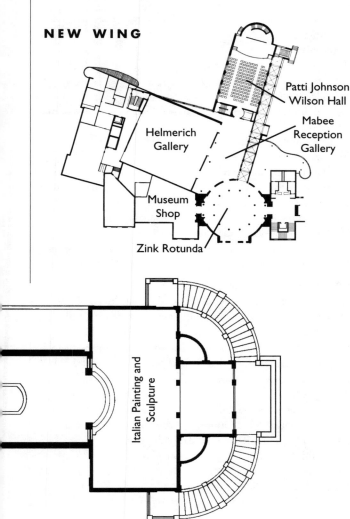

Patti Johnson Wilson Hall

Mabee Reception Gallery

Helmerich Gallery

Museum Shop

Zink Rotunda

Italian Painting and Sculpture

PHILBROOK

HOURS: Tuesday through Saturday from 10 to 5, Sunday from 1 to 5, and Thursday evening until 8 p.m. Closed Monday and legal holidays.

ADMISSION: Free to members and children 12 and under; $2.00 for students with I.D. and senior citizens; and $4 for adults. No charge to enjoy the grounds; picnicking is allowed in the open lawn areas.

TOURS: Tours can be arranged by calling (918) 748-5309 with two weeks notice.

RESTAURANT: Open Tuesday through Sunday for lunch and Sunday brunch from 11 to 2. To make reservations, call 748-5367.

LOCATION: The museum is located at 2727 South Rockford Road, one block east of Peoria Avenue at the end of 27th Street. **For more information, call 749-7941.**

OLD MEETS NEW

The architects of the new addition, Urban Design Group of Tulsa and Michael Lustig & Associates of Chicago, used the tempietto and the main entrance gate to create the major axis line of the new addition. From the front, the new wing looks like it runs on a horizontal line from the original villa. Because the architects did not want to overpower the original villa, they created more space by angling the wing toward the tempietto and adding a lower fourth story out of the natural inclination of the hill. Other innovations to look for in the addition include the copper roof over the rotunda that matches the roof of the tempietto, Kasota stone in the new addition from the same quarry as the stone in the villa, the same proportional system in both the villa and the new wing, and roof tiles on the new wing from the same firing as those on the villa, salvaged from a razed Kansas City church.

To produce the glittering effect in the otherwise flat surface, finely ground marble was used instead of the usual sand. The stone surrounding the entrance and at the wall junctions is Kasota limestone from Minnesota (the American equivalent of travertine marble). The same kind of limestone is used throughout the villa for enrichment of walls, doorways, windows, and floors. The roof of oversized Italianate tiles has wide, bracketed eaves.

Original entrance to Villa Philbrook

On the original villa the relatively small front entrance, characteristic of a Renaissance city dwelling, acts both as a barrier to the outside world and as a gate to the villa and its gardens. The purpose of the Renaissance villa was hospitality, and after entering the foyer, the villa's welcome is extended through the Great Hall to the gardens outside. This original entrance is no longer used; return to the main entrance and enter the Zink Rotunda.

ROTUNDA. Once inside the rotunda your eyes are immediately drawn to the oculus (eye) in the ceiling. The design of the space has its roots in the most important structure that still remains from ancient Rome—the Pantheon. It, too, has the oculus, but in the Pantheon it is open to the elements with a drain in the center of the floor to allow water to run off. Look through the glass door toward the back of the museum. Through the trees you can see the tempietto, a little temple used to house gods and goddesses in ancient Greece and Rome.

In the center of the rotunda is *Adam* by Rodin. On long-term loan from the Kasser Foundation in Montclair, New Jersey, this life-size bronze piece is one of only twelve in the world cast since August Rodin's death in 1917. Rodin credited Michelangelo as influencing his style. Originally, Rodin designed the Adam figure for his *Gates of Hell*.

SHOP. Before you enter the villa, you might want to visit the museum shop and purchase one of the guide books to the villa. The collection is on three floors of the villa. This tour will emphasize the main floor featuring the restored rooms and European collections.

HELMERICH WING. Walk toward the villa through the Helmerick Wing doorway. The first gallery is the **Salon Gallery.** The majority of paintings here were given to the museum in 1947 by Laura A. Clubb, who taught in a one-room sod schoolhouse in Indian Territory from 1889-91. When oil was discovered on the Clubb's ranch, she and her husband divided the oil revenues equally and pursued their respective interests. After Laura Clubb paid $12,000 for *Two Cows in a Pasture*, by Emile Van Marcke, Mr Clubb remarked, "I could have bought a train load of cattle for that!"

This gallery, which consists of many nineteenth-century French Academic paintings, was originally the kitchen and pantry of the villa. Altered in 1991 to give the aura of a French Salon (the annual exhibition sponsored and juried by the Academy), this gallery houses one of the most popular paintings at Philbrook, *The Shepherdess*. It was painted in 1889 by William-Adolphe Bouguereau (1825 - 1905), a leader in French academic painting during the second half of the nineteenth century. Bouguereau used his brush as if it were a pencil, filling in the spaces with indiscernible brush strokes. He once said, "Every detail of a work must be thought out beforehand, down to the last particular." *The Shepherdess* is a personification of the "Victorian" look with its glassy, slick perfection associated more often with china painting. The handsome young woman is depicted as a princess with delicately tapered fingers and classical bare feet. She gazes directly and serenely at the spectator; no matter where one moves, her eyes seem to follow the viewer. Toward the end of his career, Bouguereau was aware of stylistic differences between his work and that of the avant-garde artists, such as the Impressionist painters. His reputation with collectors began a steady decline during the twentieth century, but recently Bouguereau has been reappraised as a highly capable artist, representing the last breath of the long tradition

RENAISSANCE INSPIRATION

Everywhere attention to detail reflects Renaissance inspiration. Griffins and other ancient motifs on the ceiling in the hall were modeled after authentic Italian ceiling decorations of the 16th century. Painted on canvas by Cooper and Gentilomo, New York mural decorators, the canvas was then glued to the ceiling. Age spots were applied to the new paint to add interest. Roughened plaster walls suggest the imperfect plaster of early Roman architects. The serpentine columns, reminiscent of those designed by Baroque architect Bernini, relieve the unbroken expanse of the main hallway without destroying the sense of space, but more importantly they mask the 20th-century technology of steel supports hidden within their ornate twining of grape leaves.

descended from the Italian High Renaissance painter Raphael.

When you have finished viewing the artworks in this area, walk into the little room to your left that was the original breakfast room. Now it is the **Starr Collection of Wedgewood.** (Martha Jane Starr, the donor along with her husband John, is Waite Phillips's niece.)

Through the other door is the **English Portrait Gallery,** formerly the Italian formal dining room. When the villa was turned into a museum in 1938, the original wooden-coffered ceiling was removed and reinstalled upstairs in Mr. Phillips's bedroom, now the Chinese Gallery. During the 1991 restoration, the original marble fireplace was reinstalled. This gallery features a display of miniature paintings as well as portraits by two well-known American colonial painters who made their careers in England, John Singleton Copley and Benjamin West.

Across the hall is one of the most inviting rooms at Philbrook, the walnut-panelled library. Phillips often entertained his friends in this room. The colorful globe lamp, fashioned for the house, is after a map by Leonardo da Vinci. The ceiling is select gum timber, the floor is red oak, and the fireplace is Italian marble. The grandfather clock was a gift to one of George Washington's generals, Anthony Wayne. Look for his name and picture engraved on the clock, made by David Rittenhouse, a noted Philadelphia clock maker. Now endowed in honor of Robert J. LaFortune, the **Library/Founders' Room** houses temporary exhibitions relating to the history of the residence and its collections. Before leaving, notice the portraits of Waite and Genevieve Phillips. The portraits were commissioned at the time the Phillipses donated their home.

Return to the hall and walk toward the original foyer. Long expanses of open space in three directions invite you to pause, yet encourage you to explore farther. When Will Rogers first saw the entrance hall set off by the splendid ornamental iron and bronze grills and two broad flights of stairs, he said, "Well, I've been to Buckingham Palace, but it hasn't anything on Waite Phillips's house."

Stepping down into the **Great Hall** you can note the only evidences of the roaring twenties are the iron-work railings

Across the hall is one of the most inviting rooms at Philbrook, the walnut-panelled library. Phillips often entertained his friends in this room. The colorful globe lamp, fashioned for the house, is after a map by Leonardo da Vinci.

depicting flappers. But to take you back 500 years to the Italian Renaissance, plaster ceiling beams were painted with distress marks, and the lights are Venetian lantern fixtures. Opposite the fireplace wall are pierced plaster screens, which allow the sounds of the pipe organ to filter through the room. Delay the urge to go outside to the gardens and continue viewing the museum.

Return to the hall and walk to the south end of the villa. On your left is the **Italian Room,** once the living room, furnished in the style of a sixteenth-century palace. Typical of an Italian palace, the gold embellished coffered ceiling is high, and the walls are hung with rich silk damask. The elaborate ceiling reflects Baroque influence. The folding desk (a vargueno), originally made for the storage of jewels and valuable papers, is ornamented with colorful enamel plates relating the story of St. Ursula. Seventeenth-century Roman candlesticks are in the shape of twisted Corinthian columns. Before you leave the room, notice ancient molding motifs surrounding the fireplace and the doorway.

An interesting juxtaposition in style is the small **Music Room** across the hall. An example of a 1920s period piece, the room is decorated with a wall mural depicting bobbed-hair flappers wearing Grecian garb in a mythical setting. This mural was painted by George Gibbs of Philadelphia. The classical figures, used to illustrate the four movements of a symphony (allegro, rondo, andante, scherzo), represent gods in Greek and Roman mythology. The scene on the left wall symbolically blends Apollo, who played the lyre, and Dionysus, who was often seen with his leopards. The three young ladies on the opposite wall are a reminder of the Three Graces, and scattered around the room are satyrs, companions of Dionysus recognized for their love of music. The musical motif is continued on the capitals of the columns flanking the entry. Now this room houses Decorative Arts. (Before you leave, look for a resemblance between Genevieve Phillips and the figure depicted near Apollo.)

Step down into the former **sun room,** originally featuring casual furniture of the twenties. The Phillipses usually began

The Phillipses usually began their smaller parties in here with cocktails and ended by dancing on the glass dance floor. The distinctive floor (under the area rug), with its alternating colored lights, was copied from one seen by Mrs. Phillips in a famous Parisian nightclub. Today this room and the next three rooms house the Italian Painting and Sculpture Collection.

KEEPING COOL

The graceful fountain piece in the south end of the Villa, *Joy of Waters,* was designed by Harriet Frismuth, a leading American sculptress. The running water of the fountain functioned both aesthetically and practically—the soothing sounds psychologically cooled the spirit while providing a cool respite from Oklahoma heat before the days of air conditioning. Behind the fountain in the former south terrace room is a companion piece, *Call of the Sea,* also designed for the house by the same artist. Both this room and the next were originally open to the outside; architect Edward Buehler Delk, with his innovative design and placement of the villa on the land, took advantage of the prevailing Oklahoma winds. The former south terrace was furnished for leisure with large hassocks and chaise lounges.

their smaller parties in here with cocktails and ended by dancing on the glass dance floor. The distinctive floor (under the area rug), with its alternating colored lights, was copied from one seen by Mrs. Phillips in a famous Parisian nightclub. Today this room and the next three rooms house the Italian Painting and Sculpture Collection. The first gallery displays Sienese and Florentine works from the Proto-Renaissance era. During the 1300s in Italy, the first movements of humanism began to appear in works by Duccio, a Sienese painter, and Giotto, a Florentine painter. They began to give their saints weight and character, freeing them from the highly symbolic Byzantine style, characterized by stiff figures against a heavily gilded background. The *Madonna and Child* by Taddeo di Bartolo is a beautiful example of Sienese style, which combined Byzantine and Gothic characteristics.

Today all the paintings in the next gallery are by artists active in Venice during the late fifteenth and sixteenth centuries, the "golden age" of the Venetian Renaissance. In contrast to the Florentine works whose artists emphasized line and form, the Venetian artists emphasized light and color in a poetic way. In Giovanni di Giacomo Gavazzi's *Madonna and Child,* you can see a stylistic change in the portrayal of baby Jesus. Here the child is much more child-like with proportions that better emulate a baby than in the earlier works from the previous room. During the Renaissance, artists

Madonna and Child

became interested in portraying people as they actually appeared in life, rather than an idealized conception of humans.

Now step down into the next room and look to your right for the large altarpiece by Biagio d' Antonio da Firenze of *Adoration of Child with Saints and Donors,* a superb piece from the Kress Collection. Painted about 1476 for the church of St. Michele in Faenza, it portrays the donor, nobleman Ragnoli, in the extreme left next to his son; his wife is on the extreme right. (They are the only major figures without halos.) The altarpiece is particularly wonderful in its use of symbolism and in its accurate depiction of the city of Florence as it appeared in the 1470s. A curious structure in ruins is surrounded by St. Christopher carrying the baby Jesus (on the left), St. Sebastian being shot with arrows by the Roman army (on the right), Mary, Jesus, John the Baptist (a child in a camel-hair garment), and other saints. The crumbling building symbolizes the end of the pagan era and the beginning of the Christian era. (Once you recognize some of the attributes of the saints—arrows piercing St. Sebastian, St. John's reed staff and hair shirt—it is interesting to discover these saints in other Renaissance paintings.)

Before you leave this area, enjoy the Baroque works at the opposite end and the sculpture pieces in the last gallery with its view to the south lawn. This terrace ended in a pair of wide staircases descending to the evergreen allee that leads to the summerhouse.

Main staircase and landing. Return to the hall and walk to the stairs. Flanking Philbrook's main staircase are two eighteenth-century Flemish tapestries. On your left is *The Marriage of Psyche and Eros;* opposite is *Psyche at her Toilette.* The gods are identified by their attributes: Zeus with his thunderbolts and eagle, Hera with her peacock, Poseidon with his trident. Venus, Eros's mother, is centrally located between the wedding pair. Designed for the Empress Maria Theresa, the tapestries were later presented as a wedding gift to the fifth son of George III of England. Phillips purchased them after World War I.

Above the landing is a stained glass window made by D'Ascenzo Studios of Philadelphia depicting fourteenth-century poet Dante and his unattainable Beatrice.

Column in the Great Hall, in the style of Bernini

Upstairs. At the top of the stairs are bedrooms converted into gallery space. On your right at the end of the hall is the Chinese gallery, formerly Mr. Phillips's bedroom. The fireplace, original to Philbrook, is copied after one in the home of Spanish painter El Greco. The painted walnut ceiling was originally in the Phillips's formal dining room.

For an excellent view of the grounds, walk across the hall to the room housing **Asian pottery.** At the end of the room, formerly Mrs. Phillips's bedroom, the door on the left leads outside to the balcony. (This is a particularly wonderful view of the grounds for the handicapped. The grounds are explained later in the tour.)

Basket by Datsolalee, Louisa Keyser

Ground floor. After viewing the art works upstairs, return to the Great Hall downstairs and find the stairs next to the fireplace that lead to the ground floor. Gallery space for **Native American and African works** was created from the Phillips's several Western and Indian-styled club rooms. The **Santa Fe Room** contains the Oscar Berninghaus painting of Philmont, formerly the Phillips's 127,000-acre ranch in Cimarron, New Mexico. They donated it in 1941 to the Boy Scouts of America. This room is decorated with furniture formerly owned by the Phillipses.

East terrace. When you have finished viewing the villa and art works, return upstairs and proceed outside to the fountain on the **east terrace.** From here you have a wonderful view of the formal gardens, the reflecting pools, and the **tempietto.** The twenty-three acres of landscaped grounds complement the villa by carrying its decorative scheme outside. The twisted columns that mirror those in the hall are at the far end of the formal gardens and frame the tempietto below. Both fountains echo the many fountains of the villa. A **water chain** (rill), the axis of the upper gardens, is a convention used during Renaissance times to create a pleasant atmosphere of sight and sound for dining outdoors and a clever place to cool wine. Symmetry and balance, evidenced in parterres (the triangular beds of English boxwood that enclose zoysia grass), reproduce the themes of proportion and harmony essential to the design of the villa. Even the expansive vista of the grounds is an extension of the view first encountered after entering the original villa. The design of the gardens reflects the intent of the Renaissance gardens of a sixteenth-century country house—to create a place of tranquility and beauty inviting one to contemplate and to restore body and soul.

Waite Phillips habitually put his initials on many of his buildings (Downtown Walk I), and Philbrook is no exception. Look for the "WP" carved in the stonework of the balustrade on either side of the fountain and on the top railing of the loggia (porch) behind you. On both sides of the villa's doorway are two bas-relief stone panels of classical influence that reiterate the Music Room's theme. To the left is Dionysus accompanied by Maenads; to the right are Greek musicians, whose central figure is strongly reminiscent of Orpheus, the Greek god of song. The griffin chairs complete the classical theme.

Before you leave the terrace walk to the north end (left if you are facing the gardens) and view the exterior of the new addition. Notice the curved glass wall of the restaurant and, next to the auditorium, the loggia that replicates the dimensions of the east terrace loggia. Below is a sculpture garden.

Kpelie mask, Senufo, Ivory Coast

Leave the terrace by walking down the steps to the north and discover a faun, playfully holding an infant, hidden in a stone niche. He is crowned with grape leaves. His companion piece, a nymph holding a child and bedecked with flowers, is on the opposite side of the garden stairs. The figures are quite appropriate to the villa and introduce a delightful note of levity in the formal setting. At one time the bronzes were used in the gardens of the Maison Marchande estate near Paris.

Gardens. Continue walking through the formal gardens. Providing a screen between the new and formal gardens is a planting of unusual trees for Oklahoma, columnar English oaks.

REFLECTING POOLS

Farther along the path are the informal gardens reflecting English eighteenth-century tastes. The larger pool was originally an irregularly shaped swimming pool. Take time to enjoy the many varieties of plantings surrounding the pools. (Be careful not to stand on the loose rocks.) Each season offers a new array of flora. In spring, a blaze of color is achieved with flowering quince and salvia. In summer, begonias, marigolds, and salvia are bordered by ageratum and alternamthum and highlighted by standard specimens of tropicals such as lantana, hibiscus, copperleaf, and chenille.

These trees are very slow growing and suggest tight, column-like Italian cypress trees.

At the bottom of the next set of stairs, you will find a pleasant surprise—an American-styled **rock garden** completely hidden from view when you are standing on the east terrace.

Walk to the **tempietto,** built on top of a mound, originally containing dressing rooms for the Phillipses and their friends. Modeled after an ancient Greek or Roman temple built to house a god or goddess, the tempietto is an indication of the interest in the classical past found in English gardens. Stand inside and notice the image of the villa in the reflection pool. During the Renaissance, many villas were built without bedrooms because they were used solely for daytime excursions. On this villa the second floor is de-emphasized.

Behind the tempietto is **Crow Creek,** a gentle brook running through the grounds and lending itself to Philbrook's name. During the building of the estate, the creek's channel was routed and stabilized. Hand-cut sandstone rocks were used to line the creek bed (a project that took two years), and numerous berms were formed from soil obtained from the new channeling of the brook.

Across the creek is a small grotto area that once housed a **barbecue pit.** The remainder of the twenty-three acres consists of open lawns, wooded areas, and greenhouses (to the north), where the Philbrook gardeners grow most of the plantings. Along with the many native oaks, hickories, and sycamores is one of the largest atlas cedars growing in Oklahoma. The magnolias, planted by Waite Phillips for his wife, Genevieve, are believed to be the oldest in Tulsa. Sprinkled about are red buckeye, Chinese chestnut, and many trees native to Oklahoma such as redbud, river birch, black walnut, and pecan.

Before leaving the tempietto, consider how thoroughly villa Philbrook represents the Italian Renaissance. Better than any other age, the Renaissance understood what nature and art, harmoniously integrated in a villa and garden, could offer to restore man's soul from worldly cares, and Philbrook successfully reflects this philosophy. From this view the villa, with its balconied loggia, symmetrical design, and elongated silhouette atop a hill, looks as though it belongs in the hills of Italy.

Gilcrease

Gilcrease scores for vision. Part Indian, living out there in Oklahoma, and coming just after the first wave of big-gun collectors, he wisely steered clear of European old masters and went ahead to amass the most impressive collection of American paintings and Indian art in this country.

THOMAS HOVING
Connoisseur, 1983

I N 1983 THOMAS HOVING, renowned art critic and author, ranked Thomas Gilcrease twenty-first among some three hundred American collectors. Gilcrease, founder of The Thomas Gilcrease Institute of American History and Art, placed well ahead of such famous collectors as Armand Hammer and J. Paul Getty. The Institute, now popularly known as Gilcrease Museum, is primarily the product of Gilcrease's work over a period of approximately twenty-five years.

In the years between the late 1930s and 1962, the year of his death, Gilcrease collected more than 10,000 art works, more than 250,000 Indian artifacts, and more than 100,000 books and rare documents. (Such documents include a letter of 1512, believed to be the oldest surviving letter written from the New World, dictated and signed by Diego Columbus, son of Christopher Columbus. Another letter by Diego, written in 1519, includes the first reference to the introduction of blacks into America as slaves. In addition, Gilcrease has the only surviving certified copy of the Declaration of Independence, a letter written by Thomas Jefferson in July of 1776 forecasting this document, and the Articles of Confederation signed by Benjamin Franklin.)

Many things combined to bring this collection to fruition. Gilcrease's pride in his Creek heritage strongly influenced his interest in North American art, documents, and artifacts. His financial success in oil and banking, beginning with the discovery of oil on his property in the famous Glenn Pool district when he was only fifteen, provided the means to pursue collecting. Extensive traveling in Europe sparked his interest in pre-

TIME

1.5 hours

GILCREASE

LOCATION:
Gilcrease Museum is located at 1400 Gilcrease Museum Road, less than five minutes from downtown Tulsa. The fastest route is the Gilcrease Museum Road exit off Highway 64/51. Go north approximately one mile, crossing Edison Street and then West on Newton Street. The museum will be on your left. For this tour the best place to park is the parking lot on the south side of the museum.

HOURS: Gilcrease Museum is open from 9 to 5, Monday through Saturday and until 8 p.m. on Thursday. Sunday and holiday hours are 1 to 5 p.m. Between Labor Day and Memorial Day, the museum is closed on Mondays. It is also closed Christmas Day. Admission is by voluntary donation, with suggested amounts of $3.00 for individuals and $5.00 for families.

TOURS: Guided tours are conducted at 2:00 p.m. every day, or special tours can be arranged by calling the tour coordinator at (918) 596-2705.

LIBRARY: The library is open for research by appointment.

MUSEUM SHOP: Open during regular museum hours.

RESTAURANT: The Rendezvous Restaurant serves from 11 a.m. to 4 p.m. Tuesday through Saturday, specialty entrees from 5 to 8 on Thursday, and brunch from 11 to 3 p.m. on Sunday.

serving America's culture, and professional advice from distinguished art experts and artists provided the guidance necessary to amass this strong and cohesive collection of American art.

Gilcrease once said, "It is my intention to make real the true story of our own land." Believing that students could "best learn of their own past" and "of their country through . . . paintings, sketches and manuscripts," Gilcrease opened his collection to the public in 1949. By 1954, however, mounting debts forced the sale of the entire collection. Subsequently, an unusual transaction occurred between the city of Tulsa and Gilcrease. Tulsans overwhelmingly approved a $2.25 million bond issue which purchased the collection, with Gilcrease generously assigning royalties from his Texas oil properties to pay the city's debt.

The original museum structure was built in the style of an Indian longhouse. The $12.25 million, three-story expansion and renovation project which opened in November of 1987, doubled the exhibition space and allows approximately 20% of the collection to be on view at any one time.

Throughout the grounds picnic tables and benches are spaced for relaxation and picnicking. A gazebo is located in Stuart Park, an ideal place for a picnic. Because the trail involves a little climbing, wear non-slip shoes.

TULSA HISTORICAL SOCIETY MUSEUM. The best way to experience

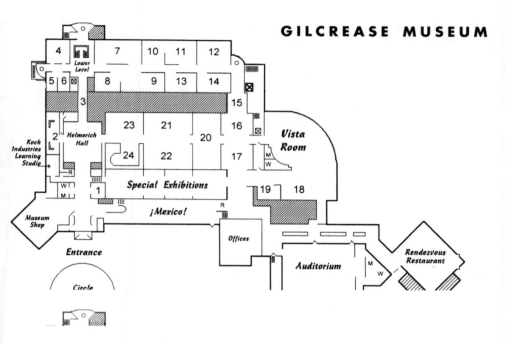

GILCREASE MUSEUM

Gilcrease Museum is to first visit Thomas Gilcrease's home, which now houses the **Tulsa Historical Society Museum,** which exhibits works that highlight specific aspects of its collections and is the business office for the organization. Currently, Gilcrease's grounds of 440 acres consist of large tracts of woods and meadows, including Stuart Park and its two ponds. Twenty-three of the acres adjacent to the museum are landscaped with four historic theme gardens that reflect the museum's collection. Each garden is true to its respective era in the use of plant material, fencing, and arrangement of flower beds, paths, and hedges. The **theme gardens** include Pre-Columbian, Colonial, Pioneer, and Victorian. Other gardens include the Rock Garden at the south entrance, the Friendship Garden by Gilcrease's **Mausoleum,** the Gillie Garden (honoring the muse-

TULSA HISTORICAL SOCIETY MUSEUM

LOCATION: On the grounds of the Gilcrease Museum.

HOURS: 11 to 4, Tuesday, Wednesday, Thursday, and Saturday, and from 1 to 4 on Sundays.

THE HOME OF THOMAS GILCREASE

Gilcrease purchased his home, built for attorney Flowers Nelson in 1913-14, in 1914, primarily because of the spectacular views. Standing in the Victorian Garden's gazebo and looking to the southeast, you have a wonderful view of the Tulsa skyline; to the northwest are the beautiful Osage Hills.

Gilcrease had an affinity for the land. He loved to work among his plants, and one day some young people who were visiting the museum, mistaking him for a gardener, asked, "Is this man Gilcrease alive?" He stopped his work, pinched himself, and answered, "Yes, he's still alive." Many of the trees and shrubs on this site were planted during Gilcrease's lifetime.

um volunteers) by the front entrance, and the Vista Garden close to the entrance of Stuart Park on the north side of the museum. The gardens are kept seasonally beautiful by the City Parks Department with masses of spring bulbs, including thousands of daffodils, and numerous shrubs, trees, and perennial and annual flowers. (For a map and more information on the gardens, check at the front desk of the museum.)

After enjoying the Victorian Garden and the inside of Gilcrease's home, stroll by Gilcrease's mausoleum on the way to the museum entrance. In front is the monumental *Sacred Rain Arrow* by the late sculptor Allan Houser. The great nephew of Apache chief Geronimo, Houser was born in Oklahoma in 1914 near Apache. When he was ten, his family moved to New Mexico. At twenty he studied under Dorothy Dunn at the Santa Fe Indian School, where he received an award in 1936 for the best artwork by a student. That same year he painted a mural for the World's Fair in New York City. Former Gilcrease Museum director Joan Carpenter Troccoli explains, "Houser was one of the pioneers who took American Indian art away from the margin and brought it into the mainstream. He was able to absorb the ideas of Modernist art—people such as Henry Moore—and incorporate them into his own work, to create a distinct and individual body of work.

Works by Houser in Tulsa are in the Philbrook Museum of Art, and his sculpture *Where Friends Meet* is at University Center at Tulsa. *As Long as the Waters Flow* stands at the entrance of the State Capitol Building in Oklahoma City. Other pieces are in the Metropolitan Museum of Art in New York City and in the British Royal Collection. (His son Bob Haozous's sculpture, *Artificial Cloud,* is discussed in the Greenwood Walk.)

Inside the museum is a variety of informational materials at the Greeter's Desk on your left. Pick up a museum floor plan or use this map to guide you to your favorite objects, remembering that a sign of a living museum is change.

Down the hall from the front door, descend the steps to **Helmerich Hall.** The massive size of the hall dictates that large paintings be displayed. One of them is *Crucified Land* by the late Tulsa artist Alexander Hogue. (Visit Philbrook Museum for his *Mother Earth Laid Bare*.) Other paintings include representations of the Taos Society of Artists, such as *Superstition* by Edward Blumenschein, as well as works by Joseph Henry Sharp, E. Martin Hennings, Walter Ufer, and Bert Phillips.

Later, after viewing the exhibits in Gallery 2, return to Helmerich Hall and turn left to enter the corridor that displays works by **Oklahoma Native American Artists (3)**.

At the end of this gallery travel down the stairs (or by elevator) to view the **Visible Artifact Storage**. This area was created so that a representative selection of artifacts from the museum's immense collection could be displayed. (Permanent storage contains some twenty times the number of objects on display.) Low light levels in this area help preserve the artifacts. The breadth of items on display is truly amazing. Pottery, baskets, jewelry, pipes, beadwork and much more—including a mastodon tooth!—are arranged by time period and region. Beginning at the right side of the doors to the library and travelling around the room, you can view prehistoric and pre-Columbian artifacts, pieces from the time of the mound builders (including items from Spiro, Oklahoma), and works by Southwestern, Northeastern, and Plains Indians.

After returning upstairs, turn to your right and walk to the hall where **American Art Before the Mid-Nineteenth Century (4)** is displayed. Englishman Sir Joshua Reynolds, one of the few non-American artists in the Gilcrease collection, is represented by his painting of a Cherokee chief. The red cloak and medals worn by the chief were presented to him in the name of King George III of England in an attempt to buy his good will. Another memorable painting is John Welsey Jarvis's *Black Hawk and His Son, Whirling Thunder*. Taken east as prisoners, Black Hawk was eventually sent home when he began to upstage President Jackson. He is recorded as saying to the President, his captor, "I am man and you are another."

Continue into the big room behind the wall of paintings to view more paintings from this era. Here you will find an early portrait by John Singleton Copley and two famous paintings by Charles Wilson Peale, Presidents James Madison and George

Black Hawk and His Son Whirling Thunder, John Wesley Jarvis

Washington. The Madison portrait is famous because it depicts Madison informally, without a wig, before he was president. Several people in the White House have wanted the original painting, including Jacqueline Kennedy and President George Bush. Neither one received the original, but the museum sent a full-size photo reproduction to Washington, D. C. so Bush could use it as background for his portrait. The National Trust promptly lost it; another copy had to be sent by overnight mail.

Nearby is *Penn's Treaty* by Benjamin West. Both Copely and West were expatriates who found it necessary to travel to Europe to study the old masters and then established their careers in London. Peale also traveled to London and spent three years there studying in West's studio. He did not, however, make his career there; he chose to live in America. He became the progenitor of a notable family of American artists, the founder of the first public museum in the United States, in Philadelphia, and a sponsor of archaeological excavations. His painting of Washington is one of seven; he painted him more than any other artist. Before you leave this gallery, notice the oil *Wild Turkey* by naturalist John James Audubon. Both he and Benjamin Franklin advocated the turkey as our national symbol.

Across the hall are two galleries devoted to individual artists. The works of **Alfred Jacob Miller (5)** depict the Rocky Mountain fur trade and historic Rendezvous. The **John Mix**

Stanley gallery (6) holds portraits, western landscapes, and genre (everyday life) scenes.

Return to the stairs and walk behind Thomas Moran's seascape to enjoy the lovely view of the Osage Hills.

The next gallery is **American Art Since Mid-Nineteenth Century** (7). Near the end of his career, Gilcrease collected one typical work by a number of American artists who were not specialists of the West. This gallery includes works by William Merritt Chase, Winslow Homer, George Inness, Eastman Johnson, and James McNeill Whistler.

One of the finest and most valuable paintings in the Gilcrease collection is the life-size portrait of Frank Hamilton Cushing, completed in 1895 by Thomas Eakins. Cushing, a renowned Smithsonian anthropologist and early student of the American Indian, lived with the Zuni Indians for four and one-half years. In his studio, Eakins depicted Cushing dressed as a member of the Zuni secret society, standing in a replica of a room where Cushing probably lived while with the Zuni. In this painting notice Eakins's attention to detail and devotion to realism. Such things as Cushing's shield decorated with the image of a Zuni war god and a bandolier bag hang on the wall. Cushing is holding a war club in his right hand and a war-plume of sacred prayer feathers in his other hand. His necklace, earrings, and belt made from silver and turquoise are symbols of power and wealth. After viewing this work in the early 1980s, Sherman Lee, former director of the Cleveland Museum of Art, stated, "Seeing this painting is worth coming to Oklahoma." Opposite this work is Ridgeway Knight's *Rural Courtship,* the first painting Gilcrease purchased.

Across the hall, you can view breathtaking landscapes by **Albert Bierstadt, Thomas Moran, and George Catlin** (8 & 9). Bierstadt, schooled in Germany and one of

One of the finest and most valuable paintings in the Gilcrease collection is the life-size portrait of Frank Hamilton Cushing, by Thomas Eakins.

the leading exponents of the American Romantic style, translated beautiful vistas into grand, operatic views of the West. Sierra *Nevada Morning* is Bierstadt's major painting in the Gilcrease collection.

Moran is sometimes called the father of our national parks because his paintings were instrumental in Congress's decision to make Yellowstone the first national park in 1872. When Moran travelled in the West, he made hundreds of watercolor sketches on site. Many art experts consider these works more interesting than his finished oils, which he completed in his studio. Gilcrease Museum owns 36 oils and 208 watercolors, some of which are displayed here. (Though they are not on view, the museum also houses rare resource documents: Moran's studio records of photographs and his identification of scenes, prices, and names of buyers.)

Cross the hallway to enter the **Remington Gallery** (10). Here you can see the highest quality oils, watercolors, black and white illustrations, and bronzes by Remington. Look for *Coming Through the Rye,* four cowboys on horseback. It is considered Remington's masterpiece in bronze. His active involvement in casting contributed to the consistently high quality of his sculptures. The museum presently owns eighteen of Remington's twenty-two subjects.

The remaining galleries in this portion of the building are devoted to **Charles Schreyvogel** (11), highlighting scenes of battle and action between government troops and Plains Indian warriors; **Charles M. Russell** (12), a self-taught artist who is famous for paintings that tell stories of the Old West and often depict colorful sunrises and sunsets; and **Joseph Henry Sharp** (13) and members of the Taos Society of Artists, which Sharp founded. Sharp was one of the first Anglo artists who settled in Taos; he was attracted to New Mexico because of the clean, crisp air and the subject matter made exotic by the Indian and Spanish influence.

The Members of the **Taos Society** (14) contains several works by Oscar Berninghaus, another Taos artist.

Catch another glimpse of the museum's wonderful view from the overlook before turning right into the **Olaf Seltzer**

Gallery (15), featuring paintings, drawings, and letters from this storyteller of the West. Notice the variety of miniatures. Dr. Philip Cole, a great collector of the West, encouraged Seltzer to paint small paintings that could fit on his crowded walls. Seltzer painted more than one hundred miniatures dealing with Montana history. Be sure to read some of the illustrated correspondence between Seltzer and his patron.

On your left, take a break in the **Vista Room**, featuring one of the most spectacular views in Tulsa—the Osage Hills (particularly breathtaking in autumn) and the gardens below. These hills were the home of the Osage Indians. As described by Washington Irving in his travels through Indian territory in 1832, the Osages were "stately fellows; stern and simple in garb and aspect. . . . Their heads were bare; their hair was cropped close, excepting a bristling ridge on the top, like the crest of a helmet, with a long scalplock hanging behind. They had fine Roman countenances, and broad deep chests; . . they looked like so many noble bronze figures."

Because they retained their mineral rights, Osage Indians became the richest tribe in the world after oil was discovered on their lands in 1901. Before leaving the Vista Room, notice the paintings of Gilcrease and his daughter, De Cygne.

Exiting at the opposite end of the Vista Room will lead you to the **Fechin gallery** (19), housing paintings and sculptures by twentieth-century Russian artist Nicolai Fechin. The paintings are on indefinite loan from the Robert S. and Grayce B. Kerr Foundation.

A bit farther and you will find **Southwest Indian Artifacts** (17), featuring pottery, weavings, jewelry, and carvings reflecting the rich Indian cultures of the American Southwest.

Double back through Gallery 17 to the **William R. Leigh Gallery** (20), which houses a recreation of the painting studio of Leigh, an important 20th-century realist. He was closely linked with Remington and Russell, and the studio illustrates his painting methods. Before painting in oil, Leigh first made detailed pencil sketches (on the drawing table), oil sketches (on the fireplace mantle), and black and white charcoal compositional drawings on canvas. On the easel is a finished work, *A*

"Their heads were bare; their hair was cropped close, excepting a bristling ridge on the top, like the crest of a helmet, with a long scalplock hanging behind. They had fine Roman countenances, and broad deep chests; . . they looked like so many noble bronze figures."

Washington Irving

ARTES DE MEXICO

The Gena Gilcrease Gallery and the Jack and Maxine Zarrow Gallery bring together Gilcrease Museum's expansive collection of Mexican art and artifacts, combined with hands-on and interactive elements. The Olmec, Aztec, Maya, and other indigenous cultures are represented in ceramics and stonework, as well as historic tribal arts, such as weavings, wooden masks, and musical instruments. A collection of Mexican fine art includes the works of Diego Rivera, Rufino Tamayo, and Juan Corea. The galleries invite an exploration of the relationships among art, language, religion, history, music, and festivals, and how art contributes to cultural and individual identity.

Close Call. Opposite the studio is Leigh's interpretation of the Grand Canyon, a favorite painting of visitors to the museum.

As you approach Helmerich Hall once again, enjoy the re-creation of the painting studio of contemporary western artist, **Olaf Wieghorst** (24).

Opposite the studio is the **Plains Indians Gallery** (23), displaying art and artifacts of the Plains Indian warriors.

Before leaving Gilcrease Museum, pay a visit to the **Museum Shop,** which contains a wide variety of books, reproductions, jewelry, and hundreds of other items related to the Gilcrease collection and American history. Most of the jewelry is made by Native Americans; the silver works come from Arizona, New Mexico, and Colorado. Most of the beadwork is made in Oklahoma. The rugs are made by the Navaho tribe and the Zapotec Indian tribe of Mexico. The pottery is made by the Southwest Indians.

Remember to pick up a brochure, *The Gardens at Gilcrease,* at the front desk. You can see the rest of the gardens on the grounds and visit Stuart Park. The park trail, located north of the lower parking lot, is very short but worth visiting. In season you will see a variety of native wild flowers and trees in bloom along with many characteristic Ozark woodland plants, which have been added to the area. The brochure lists the plants on view. This walk is especially pretty in the spring when the dogwoods and redbuds are in flower and the daffodils are on display.

Said Thomas Gilcrease, "A man should leave a track of some sort."

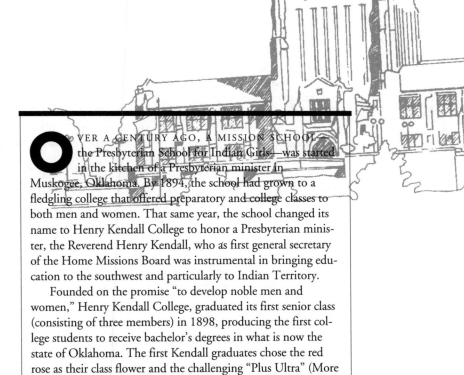

O VER A CENTURY AGO, A MISSION SCHOOL—
the Presbyterian School for Indian Girls—was started
in the kitchen of a Presbyterian minister in
Muskogee, Oklahoma. By 1894, the school had grown to a
fledgling college that offered preparatory and college classes to
both men and women. That same year, the school changed its
name to Henry Kendall College to honor a Presbyterian minister, the Reverend Henry Kendall, who as first general secretary
of the Home Missions Board was instrumental in bringing education to the southwest and particularly to Indian Territory.

Founded on the promise "to develop noble men and
women," Henry Kendall College, graduated its first senior class
(consisting of three members) in 1898, producing the first college students to receive bachelor's degrees in what is now the
state of Oklahoma. The first Kendall graduates chose the red
rose as their class flower and the challenging "Plus Ultra" (More
Beyond) as their motto.

In 1905, flushed with its success as the new "Oil Capital of
the World," "Tulsey Town" felt the need to establish creden-
tials as a progressive place to live. The Tulsa Commercial Club
(forerunner to the Tulsa Chamber of Commerce) knew that to
accomplish this task and attract the captains of the oil industry
to the city, it would be necessary to establish a university.
Coincidentally, the Presbyterian Synod, which governed the
educational and financial direction of Henry Kendall College,
was searching for a new home for the financially-troubled
school. After some wrangling, the Synod accepted the Tulsa

DISTANCE

1 mile

TIME

1 hour

THE UNIVERSITY OF TULSA

LOCATION: 600 South College Avenue, bounded by Delaware Avenue on the west, Harvard Avenue on the east, and East Fourth Place and East Eleventh Street on the north and south respectively.

PARKING: Parking on campus is allowed by permit only. However, many of the university lots also offer visitors' parking, and it is also usually easy to park on the city streets adjoining the area (East Fifth Street, South Florence Avenue, and East Fifth Place).

Commercial Club's offer of money and land, and in 1907 Henry Kendall College moved from Muskogee to Tulsa. Oklahoma had yet to become a state.

Several years later, a new college, to be named after oilman Robert M. McFarlin, was proposed for the city. Aware that Tulsa was not large enough to support two competing colleges, the Henry Kendall College trustees proposed that the contemplated McFarlin College and Kendall College affiliate under the common name "The University of Tulsa." A charter for the university was approved on November 9, 1920, and the school's name was changed in 1921 to The University of Tulsa.

On September 12, 1994, as part of its year-long Centennial Celebration, The University of Tulsa marked the 100th anniversary of the first day of classes at Henry Kendall College. Tulsa's commitment to quality higher education and continued support from the oil industry have nurtured the university's rich academic tradition. Today the University of Tulsa is the largest private university in Oklahoma.

KENDALL HALL. Begin your walk by proceeding from a small courtyard area behind **McFarlin Library.** The area, crisscrossed by sidewalks, forms a major traffic path used by students traversing the campus. The clock at the courtyard's center was given to the university by the Chi Omega Sorority to commemorate the group's fiftieth anniversary on campus. The clock's casing was cast from the mold of a clock presently found at Pont St. Michel in Paris.

Kendall Hall is the modern building directly in front of you as you face south. Its white stucco facade, raked copper roof, and expressionistic block structure, reminiscent of the architecture of Le Corbusier, is in sharp contrast with the Academic Gothic styling of the other buildings. Kendall Hall resides on the site of the original Kendall Hall, which served as the administration building for the university from 1908 until it was razed in 1972 to make way for the present structure. The new Kendall Hall houses the Faculty of Theatre, the administrative offices of the School of Music, as well as KWGS, the campus radio station and local affiliate of National Public Radio. The station's call letters are the initials of W. G. Skelly

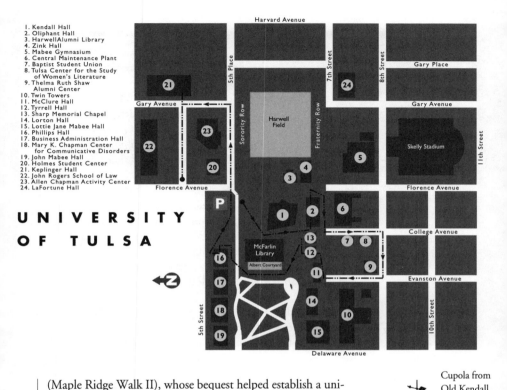

1. Kendall Hall
2. Oliphant Hall
3. HarwellAlumni Library
4. Zink Hall
5. Mabee Gymnasium
6. Central Maintenance Plant
7. Baptist Student Union
8. Tulsa Center for the Study
   of Women's Literature
9. Thelma Ruth Shaw
   Alumni Center
10. Twin Towers
11. McClure Hall
12. Tyrrell Hall
13. Sharp Memorial Chapel
14. Lorton Hall
15. Lottie Jane Mabee Hall
16. Phillips Hall
17. Business Administration Hall
18. Mary K. Chapman Center
    for Communicative Disorders
19. John Mabee Hall
20. Holmes Student Center
21. Keplinger Hall
22. John Rogers School of Law
23. Allen Chapman Activity Center
24. LaFortune Hall

U N I V E R S I T Y

O F   T U L S A

(Maple Ridge Walk II), whose bequest helped establish a university broadcasting program. The Leta M. Chapman Theatre is also housed in Kendall Hall, where the Faculty of Theatre offers year-round productions. For information about current productions, call 592-2566.

Farther south and on your left is the Statehood Bell Monument. The original bell, a gift from the First Presbyterian Church where Henry Kendall College's first classes in Tulsa were held, was rung by Mrs. Kerr, wife of the church's minister, at the moment Theodore Roosevelt signed the Oklahoma Statehood Proclamation in November of 1907. Mrs. Kerr recalled that this was the first bell to ring in Tulsa after the proclamation was made. In 1911 the bell was given to Henry Kendall College and placed in the cupola atop the original Kendall Hall. The present bell is a lighter reproduction of the 1,500 pound original.

Cupola from Old Kendall Hall

W. G. SKELLY

In 1930, W. G. Skelly gave matching funds to construct an athletic stadium. To meet his challenge, the Hurricane Club was organized to create financial support for the university's athletic programs. (Kendall College had a football team as early as 1895.) Expanded in 1947 and again in 1966, the forty-thousand seat stadium is the home field for the University of Tulsa football team and provides a playing field for local high school teams.

HALLS OF LEARNING. Continue walking south for a short distance, and just ahead on your left you will see **Oliphant Hall,** which provides classrooms and laboratories for the Faculties of Languages, Communication, and Biological Sciences as well as the Center for Student Academic Support. Oliphant Hall was initially endowed by Allen G. Oliphant, an independent oil producer, and in 1966, the Oliphant family funded the construction of the building's third floor addition.

Just before you reach Oliphant, turn east and head toward one of the oldest and one of the newest buildings on campus. The first of these will be **Harwell Alumni Library,** constructed in 1920 as the school's gymnasium which it remained until the sixties; this building now houses the Faculty of Anthropology and the Department of Information Services, the office that publishes Petroleum Abstracts, a weekly compilation of books and articles, abstracted and made available to the petroleum world.

A few steps south of Harwell you will find **Zink Hall** named after its benefactor John Steele Zink. Dedicated in 1982, Zink Hall is the home of Computing and Information Resources, the Division of Continuing Education, and the Faculty of English.

SKELLY STADIUM. Turn right and continue south briefly so that you have a broad view of **Fraternity Row** to your left and the present Athletic Gym, and **Skelly Stadium** as it bounds the campus to the south. Turn right again at this point and walk along side the university's main generator painted blue and inscribed with the symbols of the school basketball team's winning seasons.

SOUTH COLLEGE AVENUE. Directly in front of you is South College Avenue. Cross and turn left. On your right is a house occupied by the **Academic Publications Office,** including the world-renowned *James Joyce Quarterly* and *Tulsa Studies in Women's Literature,* which was founded by Germaine Greer in 1982. (Professor Greer taught at The University of Tulsa from 1979-82.)

Turn right (west) at the corner of South College Avenue and East Eighth Street and proceed to the end of the block to the Thelma Ruth Shaw Alumni Center. Built in 1977 and named for a university graduate, Thelma Ruth Shaw, the center provides a meeting hall for alumni and departmental functions. **The Shaw Alumni Center** is continuous with **Whitney Hall,** which forms the northern half of the building and houses the Office of Admission. The cupola standing in front of the center is the bell tower saved when old Kendall Hall was razed. The bell, with a frayed rope dangling from its clapper, evokes the school tradition enjoyed by graduating seniors who drop by to ring the bell for each year they attended the university.

SOUTH EVANSTON AVENUE. From here turn right and walk north on South Evanston Avenue passing the parking lot behind the alumni center building. On your left are the coed residence halls known as the Twin Towers and Twin Towers South. To your right, across the parking lot, is a building that was formerly the Baptist Student Union and is now occupied by the Office of Institutional Advancement, including Development and University Relations. To your north, directly in front of you is **McClure Hall,** which is the present administration building. Walk through the parking lot to the east of McClure Hall to **Tyrrell Hall,** which contains studios and practice rooms for the School of Music.

TYRRELL HALL. Enter **Tyrrell Hall** through the main doors on the south and ascend a short flight of stairs. To your right are heavy wooden doors that open to the hall's auditorium. If a music rehearsal is not in session, go in to view the charming, paneled room with its painted ceiling beams and Gothic arches. In the far southwest corner of the auditorium is a bronze sculpture identical to one found in the hall of Philbrook Art Center. Crafted by Adolph Weinman, whose design appears on the United Stated dime, The Duette depicts the god Pan playing his flute for a small fawn.

SHARP MEMORIAL CHAPEL. Leave the auditorium again through the wooden doors and turn right to exit Tyrrell Hall. You now have a lovely view of the main campus and the area known as the "U." Before crossing the treed plaza to McFarlin Library, stop in **Sharp Memorial Chapel,** which is directly next

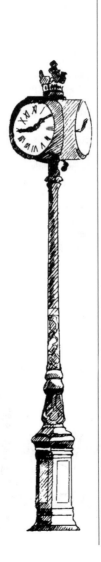

HARRY TYRRELL

In 1927, independent oil man Harry Tyrrell (Maple Ridge Walk I) announced to the university's executive committee that he planned to build a fine arts facility if other school supporters would come forth to fund other needed buildings. His offer is characteristic of the oil industry's early and continued interest in the university's future. The result was Tyrrell Hall, home of TU's School of Music.

door on your right (east). At the far end of the building, enter through the modeled bronze doors, the work of artist Bernard Frazier, former director of Philbrook Museum of Art between 1944-1950. Named after its chief donor, Robert C. Sharp, an oilman from Pennsylvania who came to Tulsa in 1917 to be Vice President of Oklahoma Natural Gas and became president of ONG in 1925, the chapel reflects the university's continued affiliation with the Presbyterian church. After a hiatus of over thirty years, voluntary chapel services for university students were reinstituted with the opening of Sharp Chapel in 1959. The stained glass windows with their brilliant jewel-like colors are filled with the images of Christ. The main panel over the altar depicts Christ as the Light of the World. Sharp Chapel is available to the public for religious services and is a popular site for weddings.

McFARLIN LIBRARY. After exiting Sharp Chapel, cross the plaza to the focal point of the campus, McFarlin Library. Walk up the stairs on your left to the courtyard level. As you look to the southwest, the building on the left just beyond Tyrrell Hall is **Lorton Hall,** which houses the Faculty of Psychology, the Graduate School and

McFarlin Library

Office of Research, and the Office of Student Financial Services. West of Lorton is Lottie Jane Mabee Hall, a women's residence. On your immediate right, at the east end of the U, is Phillips Hall, which houses the School of Art and the Alexandre Hogue Gallery. To the west of Phillips is the Business Administration Hall, home of the College of Business Administration, and farther west is Chapman Hall, which houses several departments and the administrative offices of the College of Arts and Sciences. Behind Chapman Hall, to the north, is the Mary K. Chapman Center for Communicative Disorders, which offers free screenings of speech, language, and hearing for residents of Tulsa area as well as remedial services for treatment. The Chapman Center in conjunction with the School of Nursing provides academic training in speech pathology, audiology, and deaf education. The last building on your right is John Mabee Hall which is a men's residence hall.

Straight west, Tulsa's skyline graces the horizon, providing a visual reminder of the university's multifaceted relationship to the city's past and present life. While you are in this reflective mood, find one of the benches provided in the courtyard and read further about McFarlin Library's history. Before leaving the courtyard, notice the two pieces of bronze sculpture adorning the planted areas. To the south is El Nino Volador *(The Flying Boy)* by Victor Salmones. The other work on the north side titled Primavera *(First Spring)* was donated by the local chapter of Delta Delta Delta Sorority to commemorate its fiftieth year on the university campus. The sculptor, James Michael Kelly, is a University of Tulsa graduate as is his mother, a Delta Delta Delta alumna. The children who served as models are all grandchildren of the sorority's members.

MCFARLIN LIBRARY

The imposing, towered structure built from native stone is typical of the Academic Gothic architecture that was the preferred style on most college campuses in America at the turn of the century. McFarlin Library is distinguished, however, by its innovative addition. Completed in 1979, the addition extends out from the original building and runs completely underground so as not to violate the integrity of the existing structure. McFarlin's Albert Courtyard sits atop the roof of the new addition and provides a pleasant spot from which to view the symmetry of the university's main campus.

MCFARLIN'S COLLECTIONS

Until the library's completion in 1930, library holdings were scattered among several classroom buildings, making research not only difficult but insufficient. Responding to the 1928 campus development program, Mr. and Mrs. Robert McFarlin (Riverview Walk) donated nearly $300,000 to complete the library. Over the years, the McFarlin family has continued its financial support and most recently with the subterranean addition above which you now stand.

Once the facility was completed in 1930, the library's collections grew. Alice Robertson, instrumental in the development and growth of the Presbyterian School of Indian Girls, was first to donate her collection of correspondence, photographs, and books that today are an invaluable resource for students and scholars of Oklahoma's pioneer past. Other materials

and collections ranging from Native American history and law to extensive holdings of American, British, and Anglo-Irish literature of the late 19th and 20th centuries, including the V.S. Naipaul archive, have been acquired or donated to McFarlin Library, and regularly attract visiting scholars from around the world. At present the library houses close to four million items in various formats. The Sidney Born Technical Library, established in 1961 to serve the College of Engineering and Applied Sciences, houses outstanding energy collections of more than 300,000 items pertaining to engineering and the physical sciences, making the Born Library one of the most important petroleum collections in the world. (The Born collection of glassworks is housed at Philbrook Museum of Art.)

PHILLIPS HALL. As you descend the stairs on the north side of the library courtyard, just ahead and slightly to your right is a sculpture yard that is an outdoor extension of the Alexander Hogue Gallery housed in Phillips Hall immediately to your left (west). Phillips Hall was a 1929 gift of Waite Phillips (Philbrook Museum of Art) who wished to establish a petroleum school at the university. From the thirties until the sixties, the College of Petroleum Engineering occupied the building. Phillips Hall became the School of Fine Arts when the Engineering School moved to the university's North Campus two miles away. Today, after much renovation, Phillips Hall provides studio space and classrooms for both graduate and undergraduate study in all art disciplines.

Enter Phillips Hall on the east side of the building through a small sculpture area. The **Alexander Hogue Gallery,** on the lower level where you go in, is worth visiting. The gallery's hours are from 8 until 5 weekdays, Saturday 1 until 4, closed on Sunday and all university holidays. The exhibitions are changed monthly and represent a broad spectrum of work by faculty, graduates and undergraduates, and occasionally department alumni. On the Hogue Gallery wall is a photo plaque of Adah Robinson (Downtown Walk II) who founded the University of Tulsa School of Art. The late Professor Hogue, for whom the gallery is named, directed the university's School of Art from 1945 until 1963. His international reputation began in the thirties with a series of paintings graphically depicting the water and wind erosion that plagued the southwest during the Great Depression. One of Hogue's best known works from this period, *Mother Earth Laid Bare*, is exhibited at Philbrook Museum of Art, and other works are at Gilcrease Museum.

HOLMES STUDENT CENTER. Return outside and retrace your steps through the sculpture yard. On your right, at the corner of East Fifth Place and Florence Avenue, you will see the **Holmes Student Center.** Beyond the Holmes Center, on the south side of East Fifth Place, are six sorority houses that are both meeting and living quarters for members of the national Greek associations. Sororities have been a part of campus life at the University of Tulsa since 1928.

ALLEN CHAPMAN ACTIVITY CENTER. Just northeast of Holmes is the university's newest major building, the Allen Chapman Activity Center (ACAC), which lies across the Westby parking lot and South Florence Avenue from Phillips Hall. Dedicated in 1987, and named for H. Allen Chapman, grandson of Robert McFarlin, ACAC offers cafeteria, snack bar, and coffee bar services along with the university bookstore, study and meeting space, a computer store, and other services. All meeting rooms, including the Gallery and the Great Hall, as well as the University Club, which serves as the faculty dining room, occupy the second floor.

KEPLINGER HALL. Exiting from the east end of ACAC, you will see to your left, across South Gary Place, Keplinger Hall. Dedicated in 1983 and named for a distinguished alumnus, C. H. Keplinger, the new facility brought the College of Engineering and Applied Sciences back to the main campus after twenty years. In 1959, the Humble Oil and Refining Company gave its research facility, the Jersey Product and Research Center, to the university as a gift. The gift allowed for expansion and upgraded facilities for the world-renowned Petroleum School, but also meant inconveniences for the students who took classes on both campuses. The university still

On the Hogue Gallery wall is a photo plaque of Adah Robinson (Downtown Walk II) who founded the University of Tulsa School of Art. The late Professor Hogue, for whom the gallery is named, directed the university's School of Art from 1945 until 1963.

JOHN ROGERS AND THE TU LAW SCHOOL

In the 1930s, John Rogers, then legal counselor for the McFarlin-Chapman-Barnard oil interest, presented a proposal to establish a fully accredited law school. Rogers worked tirelessly to acquire law books from local attorneys' private libraries, and in 1943, James Chapman, aware of his friend's great desire to create a fine law facility, donated $40,000 for library development. Once the new school was in operation, a faculty of full-time professors was added.

retains major research facilities on North Campus, but all classes are held in Keplinger Hall. As you enter Keplinger's west door, you will see a three-story atrium filled with natural sunlight. The atrium divides the classroom and laboratory wings, and the building with its solar collectors is completely energy efficient.

JOHN ROGERS HALL. Exit again to South Gary Place and walk north to East Fifth Street. Turn left and stroll to the next building on your right—John Rogers Hall, which houses the university's College of Law. The University of Tulsa began law classes in the twenties when it affiliated with the privately-run Tulsa Law School. The law school held classes at night in Tulsa's Court House, and courses were taught by local attorneys. Classes continued in the university's downtown school until the present building was completed in 1974, again with the major funding given by the Chapman family in recognition of John Rogers. The College of Law typically enrolls about 600 students.

When you pass John Rogers Hall, you should be in the vicinity of your car. As the University of Tulsa walk comes to an end, one realizes that the families, reading like a who's who of Tulsa's oil-rich, who helped finance these buildings greatly honored themselves in contributing to the life and promise of a university that continues to thrive and grow.

Keplinger Hall

Sites of Interest

OWEN PARK. As a point of interest today, eclipsing even its natural beauty, is Owen Park's history—quite an array of people and events.

The early 19th century saw the Osage Tribe as occupants of the area; however, in 1825 preparing for the relocation of the Five Civilized Tribes into then Indian Territory, a treaty was signed adding two additional tribes of Native Americans, the Creeks and Cherokees. A plaque just south of the fishing pond, now removed, used to mark the point where these three nations joined.

Then in 1832, fresh from the art salons in Europe, Washington Irving (Riverview Walk and Chandler Site) was an unlikely candidate to pen one of the first descriptions of the Owen Park area, and a monument with inscriptions from his book *Tour on the Prairies* is several blocks west of the park at the corner of Easton Boulevard and Vancouver Avenue. Following such successes as "The Legend of Sleepy Hollow" and "Rip Van Winkle" in the *Sketch Book,* Irving had accepted an invitation to join a government expedition through Indian Territory to Fort Gibson. About his experience he would write, "We send our youth abroad to grow luxurious and effeminate in Europe; it appears to me, that a previous tour on the prairies would be more likely to produce that manliness, simplicity, and self-dependence, most in unison with our political institutions."

Saturday, January 23, 1904 was a sad, but memorable day in Owen Park history. The nitroglycerine needed for shooting oil wells was so explosive that the railroads refused to handle it.

THE OWENS

In the 1880s, Chauncey A. Owen and his Creek wife, Martha, Owen Park's namesakes, were established as leading ranchers and farmers in the Broken Arrow region. When the railroad was extended to Tulsa in 1882, Owen contracted to supply beef and produce to the rail workers—hence establishing a new business—freighting. Next, not quite sure where the metropolis would finally settle, Owen started yet another enterprise—a moveable boarding tent, where it is said his wife's cooking became legendary. The Owens' more permanent structure, the Tulsa Hotel, a six-room, wood frame, two-story building, near present day First and Main Streets was Tulsa's first skyscraper. Martha died in 1902. Her heirs received an allotment from the Creek Nation of 160 acres, which encompassed the present Owen Park and neighborhood.

However, the Western Torpedo Company of Chanute, Kansas had 875 quarts of the substance hauled by wagon to be stored in a shed in the area. An unfortunate worker, named McDonald and substituting for a regular employee, was last seen entering the building at 4:00 p.m. carrying nitroglycerine. Fifteen minutes later a tremendous detonation shook the countryside. The blast broke the door locks at the Dr. Sam G. Kennedy (Downtown Walk I) country estate a quarter mile north and shattered glass in the business district a mile east. The boom was heard as far away as Claremore. McDonald's legacy was, perhaps, that he helped prepare the site for the future Owen Park Lake.

Today, the lake and park host a multitude of leisure time activities—picnics, strolls, concerts, and the ever popular fishing—timeless adventures from territorial days to present.

Owen Park is northwest of downtown. From downtown travel north on Denver to Edison Avenue. Turn left (west) and proceed a few blocks. Owen Park will be on your left.

RESERVOIR HILL. Reservoir Hill is the closest semblance in Tulsa to believing that you are living in San Francisco. This charming Tulsa residential neighborhood is the highest point within the city limits to be served by the Spavinaw Water System of 1924. Water from Lake Yahola is pumped to the large reservoir built into the top of the hill and then forced through lines throughout the city.

Because of its height, the hill has some of the best views of Tulsa—of downtown and the Osage Hills. The curvilinear, steep streets, and hillside homes provide a setting for 1920's adaptations of Mediterranean, Pueblo, Georgian Revival, Italianate, and several contemporary homes. The residents who live on the hill include many upper middle class families who like the convenience to downtown and relish their views, along with the friendly neighborhood cohesiveness.

Reservoir Hill is best reached by traveling north on the Osage Expressway. Take the Pine Street Exit; turn right onto Pine Street and then left onto Denver Avenue and follow the street until it "T"s at the end. From there you can go either right or left to wind your way up through the neighborhood to the top of the hill.

TRACY PARK NEIGHBORHOOD. Tracy Park is one of the closest residential areas to downtown Tulsa. In 1982 the Tracy Park Historic District was listed on the National Register of Historic Places. The neighborhood consists of approximately seventy residences built in the Ridgewood Subdivision in the early 1920s. The bungalows and two-story frame and brick houses were originally built for Tulsa's growing oil-related middle class, managers, small businessmen, and a few professionals.

Two of the homes are listed on the Oklahoma Landmarks Inventory. The **Adah Robinson House at 1119 S. Owasso** was designed by Robinson who also designed Boston Avenue Methodist Church (Downtown Walk II). She had help from her former student Bruce Goff and Joseph Koberling, the architect who designed the first Art Deco building in Tulsa, the Medical Arts Building. (Demolished in 1970, the 1926 structure once stood downtown on the site of the ONEOK parking facility.) Robinson's Art Deco home was built in 1927 and has leaded glass windows, terrazzo floors, and contemporary spaces decades ahead of its construction date. The two-story living room has an open balcony running the length of the room and a sunken conversation pit with a fireplace.

The other building listed on the Oklahoma Landmarks Inventory is, unfortunately, devoted to commercial use. The **French Cottage** on the corner of 12th and Peoria was built by William D. Jackson in 1921 with an exterior that replicated the cottage in which he was billeted during World War I.

The jewel of this area is **Tracy Park** at the corner of 11th Street and Peoria Avenue. Every spring the City Parks' Horticultural Section displays 3,000 pansies and between 10-15,000 tulips. Then in the summer and fall they plant 5,000 annuals, such as Joseph's coat, marigolds, lantana, and Mexican firebush.

Tracy Park is located on the southwest corner of Peoria Avenue and Eleventh Street.

Tracy Park is one of the closest residential areas to downtown Tulsa. In 1982 the Tracy Park Historic District was listed on the National Register of Historic Places. The neighborhood consists of approximately seventy residences built in the Ridgewood Subdivision in the early 1920s.

LOOK FOR THE ISLANDS

Other islands to look for in the area are:

UTICA AVENUE AND 22ND STREET: In memory of Nelle Shields Jackson and in honor of William F. Fisher of Miss Jackson's Shop

UTICA AVENUE AND 26TH STREET: One block west of Utica

UTICA AVENUE AND 31ST STREET

BROOKSIDE MEDIAN: On Peoria Avenue between 33rd Street and 35th Street

THE ISLANDS IN TULSA. Recently Tulsans have been busy landscaping islands in their neighborhoods. Some of the most beautiful are near Utica Avenue between 21st and 31st Streets. The first to be landscaped in this area is to the east of Utica Avenue at 27th Street and Victor. On this small plot of land, about fifteen years ago, Roxana Lorton decided to beautify this unadorned spot. She called the City Parks' Department who was thrilled to release the island to her care. Today, the island is an inspiration to others who have taken the initiative to ornament their areas. As Lorton explains, "These landscaped islands make your neighborhood look like a park."

Then, in 1987 Lorton and the late Jack Braswell decided to tackle the eyesore at Lewis and Forest Boulevard. They enlisted the help of Henry Will, Martin Wing, Kathy Coyle, Dave Collins, John Woolman, Bob Shasberger, Ron Percefull Arrowhead Landscape, and Aqua Weathermatic Sprinkler, raised $8,000 from the neighbors, and turned an unpleasant traffic island into a picturesque park with seasonal flowers. That same year "Up with Trees" validated their hard work with an award.

WESTHOPE. Westhope is one of only three Frank Lloyd Wright designed buildings (Price Tower and a private residence are in Bartlesville) in Oklahoma. Built in 1919 for Richard Lloyd Jones, Wright's cousin and owner of *The Tulsa Tribune* newspaper, the home is larger than most other Wright designed houses; it contains 10,000 square feet of floor space. Despite its tremendous size, the home comfortably accommodates only a few people or as many as 400. The two-story house has a four-car garage, garden room, shop and workroom, pool, fountain, fish pond, formal garden areas, and four patios. The building was listed on the National Register of Historic Places on July 27, 1989.

Westhope is located at 3704 South Birmingham Street, between Lewis and Harvard Avenues and between 36th and 41st Streets.

CHANDLER PARK. The craggy cliff area between Tulsa and Sand Springs that today attracts picnickers and hikers to Chandler Park still has the haunting allure that brought forth legends and intrigues associated with "Lost City." The area was called "Lost City" long before the turn of the century and, as in all good legends, the origin of the name has been lost, but several theories survive. Some say that cliff dwellers once lived here. Others say the cliff formations look like a city from the river and that early day river travelers, pushing up and down the Arkansas, coined the name. One idea is that a tiny settlement was located in the area and eventually abandoned. A 1930s account also reported that "For fifty years or more, small groups of treasure hunters have roved the craggy cliffs and rocky crevices of Lost City. Pioneers in this section say that forty years ago the report that the Jesse James Gang had hidden $88,000, wrapped in a leather cloth, among the rocks was a prevalent one. No one has ever produced a sound reason for the rumor, but to this day the search has continued from time to time."

Now 190 acres belonging to Tulsa County, the park attracts rappelling and rock climbing enthusiasts in addition to those who want to enjoy the especially wonderful views of Tulsa and the surrounding area. From the overlooks, Tulsans will recognize the much photographed profile of their city. Also, the view of the river recalls the words of Washington Irving, an earlier admirer of the Arkansas River.

Included at Chandler Park are a swimming pool, one lighted softball field, four lighted junior baseball fields, children's playground equipment, picnic tables, shelters and grills, tennis courts, restrooms, and an outdoor fitness court with basketball goals. You may reserve a shelter or the lighted softball field by calling 596-5900. (These are usually booked well in advance.) The park is the site of an Easter Pageant on the Friday and Saturday of the holiday. Near the mound where the event takes place is a frisbee golf course.

Chandler Park is open from 7 a.m. to 11 p.m. and is located at 6500 West 21st Street. (Go west on 23rd Street which turns into West 21st Street.) The park entrance is clearly marked with rock letters to the left of the road.

"It was a bright sunny morning, with a pure transparent atmosphere that seemed to bathe the very heart with gladness. Our march continued parallel to the Arkansas, through a rich and varied country;—sometimes we had to break our way through alluvial bottoms matte with redundant vegetation, where the gigantic trees were entangled with grapevine, hanging like cordage from their branches. . . . Sometimes we scrambled up broken and rocky hills, from the summits of which we had wide views stretching on one side over distant prairies diversified by groves and forests, and on the other ranging along a line of blue and shadowy hills beyond the waters of the Arkansas."

WASHINGTON IRVING, *Tour on the Prairies,* 1835

ORU

LOCATION:
7777 South Lewis
Avenue.

PARKING: Park
at the Mabee Center
(to the right after
you enter the
campus).

**VISITOR
CENTER:** The
Visitor Center,
located in the Prayer
Tower, is open
Monday through
Saturday, 10:30 to
4:30, and Sunday, 1
to 5. It is closed
Thanksgiving Day,
Christmas Eve,
Christmas Day, and
New Year's Day.
There is no
admission charge.
Private tours can be
arranged by calling
(918) 495-6807.

ORU. In an address to the first class at Oral Roberts University on September 1, 1965, Oral Roberts stated, "ORU is a daring new concept in higher education. It was planned to be from the beginning—one that would be able and willing to innovate change in all three basic aspects of your being—the intellectual, the physical, and the spiritual." Located in south Tulsa on a five hundred acre field is a $250 million university campus that continues to be one of the top ten tourist attractions in the state.

The university is a realization of a dream that evangelist Oral Roberts carried in his heart for some thirty years. Officially opened in 1965, the university now serves about four thousand full-time students representing all fifty states and numerous foreign countries. The avenue of flags at the entrance to the campus represents these nations plus the concern that ORU's graduates go out to all nations with a message of faith and wholeness. The seal, also at the entrance, contains a triangle - symbolizing the education of spirit, mind, and body - inside a circle, representing the "unified whole."

The sixty-foot sculpture of **Healing Hands,** reported to be the largest single bronze sculpture in the world, was designed by Leonard McMurry of Oklahoma City. It took two years to build the life-size and the six-foot prototypes. A sixty-foot model was cast at a foundry in Mexico City. Sections of the completed sculpture were shipped to Tulsa and reassembled piece by piece on the site. The intricate detail work can be seen in the veins and skin folds on the back of the hands and in the delicate skin creases in the palms. The hands symbolize the call given by God to Oral Roberts to unite medicine and prayer. The right hand represents the hand of prayer raised to God, the source of healing; the left hand represents the physician's commitment to place all of God's healing power in operation for every patient against every disease.

The **Prayer Tower,** referred to as the "heartbeat" of the university campus, represents the shape of a cross: the upward spire points to man's relationship with God; the outward thrust of the observation deck, to man's relationship with other men. The spikes surrounding the observation deck represent the crown of thorns worn by Jesus during His crucifixion. They are trimmed in red paint. The flame on top of the Tower is a symbol of both the Holy Spirit and evangelism. At the base of the Tower is a sunken prayer garden with three-tiered fountains and masses of seasonal foliage and flowers.

Inside the Prayer Tower are two multimedia presentations: a thirty-six minute "Journey Into Faith" tells the life story of Oral Roberts. Shows begin every fifteen minutes with the last show at 4:30. The twenty-five minute "ORU Perspective" explains the university's campus life for the past twenty-five years.

From the observation deck are spectacular views of Tulsa—of Turkey Mountain (to the northwest, left) and of downtown. Unfortunately, the "crown of thorns" is a barrier between you and an unobstructed view. The other windows offer a variety of panoramic views of Tulsa and ORU. The most prominent design themes of the campus are collections of triangles and dove-like symbols. North of the Tower on the two Roberts Halls are designs representing the cross and the descending dove worked into the gold anodized grills. Directly to the south is the Learning Resources Center, consisting of two triangles joined together to form a diamond shape.

Another building to look for is Christ's Chapel. From the Tower the chapel looks draped, an appearance reminiscent of the tents that Oral Roberts used extensively in the 1950s for the crowds that thronged to his meetings. Tulsan Frank W. Wallace, ORU's architect, notes that "My buildings have no fronts, no backs, no visible pipes or air-conditioning ducts on the roofs. I see a building as a piece of sculpture. It should be interesting no matter what the perspective of the person looking at it."

Notice how the gold glass reflects the different buildings and the ever-changing Oklahoma sky. White, blue, and gold, found on

Prayer Tower at ORU

many of the buildings, are also symbolic. White refers to wholesome living and purity, blue to truth, and gold to the riches of heaven and God.

Across 81st Street to the south is the former City of Faith, now the Cityplex. In *Time* magazine architectural critic Wolf Von Echardt's view, the City of Faith "has all of the pretentiousness, bad taste, and vulgarity of its time. It's so bad, it's good. It has guts and excitement. But, it is not my idea of building a tribute to God. God doesn't need gilded kitsch."

Both the university and the former medical complex have received a variety of comments, ranging from "absolutely beautiful" to "World's Fair." Regardless of how you judge the buildings aesthetically, it is worth noting that practically everything you see was built by contributions from Oral Robert's "partners," debt-free.

The former City of Faith, once the largest health-care facility of its kind in the world, closed in the fall of 1989. It began as a religious revelation—a vision delivered to Oral Roberts in the midst of his personal tragedy, the death of his eldest daughter, Rebecca, and her husband in a plane crash in 1977. The *Saturday Evening Post* reported, "In search of peace and relief from his grief, Roberts made a pilgrimage into the desert." There he received a message from God to build a center with " . . . an atmosphere charged with faith and hope; where My healing love fills the entire place." Given specific instructions on design and goals, including a 777 hospital bed count, Roberts proceeded to raise money for the complex. In 1978 Roberts broke ground, and today, the Cityplex, owned by ORU, houses cancer research in addition to other businesses. Patterns on the building facades reflect the Prayer Tower, a futuristic cross.

Footsteps Through Tulsa
1398 East 25th Street
Tulsa, Oklahoma 74114
(918) 749-1811 or (918) 742-3661

Please send me _____ copies of *Footsteps Through Tulsa*

_____ copies x $12.95 per copy = $_____

plus $1.50 x number of copies for postage and handling = $_____

plus $ 1.00 x number of copies for sales tax (Oklahoma residents only) = $_____

equals a total of =$_____

Amount of check: $_____
Please make checks payable to *Footsteps Through Tulsa.*

NAME _____

STREET ADDRESS _____

CITY _____**STATE** _____**ZIP** _____

DAYTIME PHONE (_____ **)** _____

....

Footsteps Through Tulsa
1398 East 25th Street
Tulsa, Oklahoma 74114
(918) 749-1811 or (918) 742-3661

Please send me _____ copies of *Footsteps Through Tulsa*

_____ copies x $12.95 per copy = $_____

plus $1.50 x number of copies for postage and handling = $_____

plus $ 1.00 x number of copies for sales tax (Oklahoma residents only) = $_____

equals a total of =$_____

Amount of check: $_____
Please make checks payable to *Footsteps Through Tulsa.*

NAME _____

STREET ADDRESS _____

CITY _____**STATE** _____**ZIP** _____

DAYTIME PHONE (_____ **)** _____